Revitalizing Undergraduate Science

Why Some Things Work and Most Don't

by Sheila Tobias

W. Stevenson Bacon, Series Editor

An occasional paper on neglected problems in science education
Published by Research Corporation
a foundation for the advancement of science

RESEARCH CORPORATION
6840 East Broadway Boulevard
Tucson, Arizona 85710-2815

Copyright 1992 by Research Corporation

Library of Congress Catalog Card Number: 92-218796
ISBN 0-9633504-1-2

To David Riesman,
Professor Emeritus of Sociology,
Harvard University,

who thinks about American higher education
with more clarity than anyone else;

And to Sanford Lakoff,
Professor of Political Science,
University of California, San Diego,

for his contribution to the clarity
of my thinking about everything.

Sources and Rapporteurs

Debbie Ashcraft, UCSD Institute
Margaret Bartlett, Fort Lewis College
Steve Brenner, Harvard University
Robert Brown, Case Western Reserve University
Brian P. Coppola, University of Michigan
Daryl Chubin, Office of Technology Assessment
Russell Doolittle, University of California, San Diego
Michael C. Doyle, Trinity University
Seyhan Ege, University of Michigan
Katya Fels, Harvard University
Therese Flaningam, UCSD Institute
David Hall, Harvard University
Sylvia Teich Horowitz, California State University, Los Angeles
Priscilla Laws, Dickinson College
David Layzer, Harvard University
Abigail Lipson, Harvard University
Eric Mazur, Harvard University
Jim Mills, Fort Lewis College
Patricia A. Moore, University of California, San Diego
Stella Pagonis, University of Wisconsin-Eau Claire
Suzan Potuznik, University of California, San Diego
Paul Saltman, University of California, San Diego
David Sokoloff, University of Oregon
Alan Van Heuvelen, New Mexico State University
K. Wayne Yang, Harvard University

Contents

Introduction

R*evitalizing Undergraduate Science: Why Some Things Work and Most Don't* makes clear why so few efforts at reforming science education are successful, and why it is that the 300 studies on the subject published over the past decade have done little more than add to a growing body of literature. It is a second Research Corporation paper on the problems of science education: declining interest in science on the part of able U.S. college students motivated a previous work, also authored by Sheila Tobias, that found that introductory college physics and chemistry are less than positive experiences for many who come to college with some talent and taste for science.[1]

Revitalizing Undergraduate Science takes us on a tour of programs (and courses) that appear successful in terms of faculty accomplishments; students graduated and entering advanced study or the professional workplace; and showing evidence of high morale among both faculty and undergraduates. These successful programs are found in places as diverse as a state university in the multicultural environment of East Los Angeles; an institution of the University of Wisconsin system in rural Wisconsin; an elite private institution in Texas; a Colorado state college; and three of the nation's great research universities.

Common elements in many of these programs are abandonment of an almost exclusive emphasis on problem solving and modification of the lecture format to permit teaching of underlying concepts. Other variations in traditional introductory physics and chemistry courses are aimed at persuading those simply fulfilling graduation requirements to major in science; at bringing minority students into the fold; or at combining physics and/or various subfields of chemistry in different ways to promote better understanding.

Harvard's "chem-phys," for example, is not only such a combination, but a case study in another dimension: how innovation–an elegant, intellectually satisfying new course–can be stymied by lack of univer-

---

[1] Sheila Tobias, *They're Not Dumb, They're Different: Stalking the Second Tier* (Tucson, Ariz.: Research Corporation, 1990)

sity-wide change. Lasting change occurs, Tobias says, when everybody wants it, when there is a passion to improve, when there is nearly universal "buy-in."

Revitalizing Undergraduate Science carries the argument forward through case studies, not as case reports selected by category or type. Although chemistry programs and courses cluster in the first half of the book and undergraduate physics courses are discussed in later chapters, some physics appears in connection with chemistry (chapter 6), and chemistry returns in chapter 9. Certain themes (not disciplines) are visited and revisited in different environments. The goal is to compare institutional responses to the challenge of teaching undergraduate science rather than to survey discipline-specific experiments.

As one example, the theme at the University of Wisconsin-Eau Claire (chapter 2), and Fort Lewis in Durango and Trinity in San Antonio (chapter 3), is continuous attention to the quality of undergraduate instruction overall, and continuous improvement of already successful programs. On the surface the University of Michigan (chapter 4) offers yet another chemistry program in transition, but the setting is larger and the theme is not so much improvement as fundamental *change*. From Michigan the argument carries us to another research institution, the University of California, San Diego (chapter 5) to consider a more modest change: enrichment of a course in chemistry for nonscience majors. This in turn leads us to "chem-phys" at Harvard (chapter 6), a multidisciplinary introduction to the physical sciences designed to challenge beginning students.

This bridge to physics introduces still another theme: the application of cognitive research to teaching. Tobias reports some of the findings of this research, then presents case studies from New Mexico State University, Dickinson College, and Case Western Reserve (chapter 7). These bring us back to Harvard and yet another model for reform of physics education (chapter 8). In chapters 9 and 10 new questions are posed: what can be done to recruit America's historically underrepresented and some of her newer minorities for science, and what are the obligations of the great research universities toward training elementary and high school teachers. The first and last chapters of this report are bookends, meant to frame the argument in both theoretical and practical ways.

As might be surmised, the programs selected for study in *Revitalizing Undergraduate Science* are neither random nor symmetrical. Tobias has used the methods of ethnography in reporting what makes individual programs interesting, what their faculty are doing, what they are *thinking about what they are doing*, and what others can learn from their experience. This is particularly appropriate since efforts to reform science education to date have demonstrated that the politics and the process of change are not well understood.

For those accustomed to doing science, Tobias' methods and measures will seem inconclusive, but the processes of change are not susceptible to exact assessment. Reform is a process rather than a scientific problem to be solved, and the perfect curricula and pedagogies may prove forever elusive. Given the transitory nature and dismal record to date of innovations in the field of science education, science and society will be the beneficiaries even if these case studies inspire only a few imitators.

John P. Schaefer
President
Research Corporation

Tucson, Arizona
May 1, 1992

1

Science Education Reform
What's Wrong with the Process?

I am seated around a conference table at an average-size comprehensive state university in the mid-South. I have come to tell the faculty in science that my research shows that the four-year state institutions, of which theirs is typical, are doing a very good job meeting undergraduates' needs in science. But these faculty are not convinced. From their vantage point students are woefully underprepared in mathematics and science, and unwilling to work hard. Money is scarce for the kinds of improvements they'd like to try. Attempts to place students in stratified introductory math courses founder on a university-imposed policy that allows undergraduates to select their own sections of a course, whatever their placement scores. My host, the dean of science, is committed to improving the quality of undergraduate instruction. But he, too, is frustrated. What makes a difference, he asks? Should he concentrate on class size? On faculty development? On courses for nonscience students? Or on grants-getting for educational projects? He is pleased when an instructor does an excellent job of teaching, but not sure how to guarantee this happens more of the time.

Up the road, at the research university in the same state, a vice president for academic affairs is also determined to do the right thing. Though not a scientist, he is convinced that science is a liberal art which ought to be integrated more fully into the undergraduate curriculum. He recently inaugurated an internal fund to encourage innovation in undergraduate science teaching. When I tell him I am not as impressed with innovation that requires special funding as with steady improvement, he invites me to give him a list of such improvements he might make.

The problem at both institutions is well understood: too few undergraduates willing to enroll and persist in science. Responsibility for changing that picture is, however, diffuse. Faculty members are involved in the undergraduate courses they teach, but no one pays much attention to the overall quality of instruction. And even if the faculty were to accept collective responsibility, how does a single department deal with budget constraints; university-wide policies inappropriate to science teaching; credit-hour formulas that do not reflect the time faculty and students spend in class and laboratory sections; poor advising; grade inflation in fields other than science; unenforced (or unenforceable) admissions requirements; and students' poor precollege preparation in science and mathematics?

Few issues are as straightforward as students' precollege preparation and grade inflation. Yet few scientists are as willing to undertake the kind of high-risk action needed to make change as the faculty at the University of Utah who voted to counter grade inflation by appending *the average grade for the course as a whole* to each student's transcript; or as the faculty senate at Louisiana State University which negotiated with the public schools to be able to insist on a year of chemistry, a year of biology, and a year of physics as a requirement for college admission. Both are the kinds of bold steps that send out clear signals. Indeed, since the new standards went into effect in Louisiana in 1988, the number of high school students taking physics has doubled, and 20 percent more physics instructors have been hired at the high school level. By compensating students who take science at Utah with honor points, calculated as the positive *difference* between a student's final mark and the average grade in the course, the university is hoping to drive down grade inflation elsewhere on campus. But knotty as such issues are, they are easier by far to tackle than the more diffuse goal of improving undergraduate science instruction overall.

The emphasis in science education reform is increasingly directed to undergraduate teaching. After many years of neglect department chairs, university administrators, policy makers and, importantly, funders are beginning to focus on the role of the introductory course in setting the tone for undergraduate science. But few approaches are as obvious as Louisiana's and Utah's attempts to deal with poor preparation and grade inflation. And what guarantees that reform at the college level–despite renewed attention and some outside funding–will be any more success- ful or long-lasting than attempts to reform precollege science education in the past?

With these questions in mind, I began a two-year quest for under- graduate science programs that work. My purpose was to locate them, study them, and try to tease out, by means of narrative case studies, what does and doesn't succeed in a variety of undergraduate settings. I was interested in both newly revised programs and those that had been in place for some time. My criteria for what works were the obvious: successful recruitment of students; a high rate of retention of those crossing the introductory threshold; and student and faculty morale.

While there is diversity in the following case studies, several things are clear: nowhere is reform the product of a "quick fix." Nowhere is an outside idea–not even an outside expert–as vital in achieving high quality instruction as local initiative and control. And, except for some programs that receive outside funding for instrumentation and undergraduate stipends, much of the best of what works is internally generated and internally paid for. All this flies in the face of the model that has dominated science education reform, and leads me to two conclusions: first, we need some new thinking about science education reform in general; second, we need to find new ways to nurture departments and faculty who are committed to lasting change.

New thinking begins with a critique of old thinking.

Ever since the launching of Sputnik thirty-five years ago Americans have been obsessed with science education reform. Task forces meet and commissions recommend, but little makes its way from the edge to the center of the educational process. What is new and different–New Math or self-paced instruction, or writing across the curriculum, or teacher competence–is initially embraced, but hard to locate only a few years later. In education there appears to be a strong default mechanism, inertia in the system that educational reform, as currently practiced, rarely diverts or modifies.

Some 300 reports on the problems of American science and mathematics education have been issued (at the rate of about one per week) since 1983. Even more startling than their frequency is their cost in dollars spent and effort expended. Yet, with certain notable exceptions such as *A Nation at Risk*[1] and *Everybody Counts*,[2] it is difficult to show that these reports have had much impact. Topics range from an "underachieving curriculum" in mathematics to regrets that science is not taught as a liberal art, to glossy pep talks intended to cheer us on to unrealistic goals ("First in the world in science and mathematics by the year 2000"[3]). Some of these documents are richer in analysis than others, particularly those dealing with the absence of women and minorities from mathematics and science.[4] Some few provide insight into the problems of reform itself in

---

[1] *A Nation at Risk: The Imperative for Educational Reform*, National Commission on Excellence in Education, U.S. Department of Education, Washington, D.C., 1983.

[2] *Everybody Counts: A Report to the Nation on the Future of Mathematics Education*, Summary, National Research Council, National Academy Press, 1989.

[3] *America 2000: An Education Strategy*, U.S. Department of Education, Washington, D.C., 1991.

[4] Marsha Lakes Matyas and Shirley M. Malcom, eds., *Investing in Human Potential: Science and Engineering at the Crossroads*, American Association for the Advancement of Science, Washington, D.C., 1991.

a nation that cherishes local autonomy at the school and college levels. But when the authors finally come around to solutions, they offer laundry lists that range from the difficult–improving teacher education–to the near impossible–changing public perceptions of mathematics and science.

Nor are the reports consistent. Certain experts advise us to worry about an anticipated "shortfall" in the numbers of engineers and scientists that will occur by the year 2000. Others deny the shortage and tell us instead that science illiteracy is our greatest problem. Who do we believe? What are we supposed to do? Where do we go for the answers?

The Case Studies

In their seminal book on higher education, published in 1968 and entitled *The Academic Revolution*,[5] Christopher Jencks and David Riesman pieced together a methodology for studying change in American higher education. They combined "hard data" where they could find it, "ethnographic studies" of several disparate institutions, and informed interpretation and speculation–a model borrowed in the preparation of this volume. Anticipating that "some readers will frown on this type of inquiry, preferring less ambitious but more fully documented analyses," i.e., a more "scientific study," Jencks and Riesman wrote in the introduction to their book:[6]

> . . . responsible scholarship must invent methods and data appropriate to the important problems of the day. To reverse this process, choosing one's problems to fit the methods and data that happen to be most satisfactory, strikes us as an invitation to triviality and ultimately as an abdication of social and personal responsibility. . . . [In this study] many facets . . . may even be scientific, in the sense that another investigator can repeat the inquiry with reasonable assurance of getting similar results. But even when the data look "hard," . . . their meaning is almost always ambiguous, subject to interpretations. . . .

Jencks and Riesman's subject was the changing relationship between higher education and American society. Mine is more modest, a description and analysis of programs and courses in which larger than expected numbers of students, including minority students, are being recruited to

---

[5] Christopher Jencks and David Riesman, *The Academic Revolution* (Garden City, N.Y.: Doubleday and Co., 1968)

[6] Ibid., p. xii.

and are staying in science. My selection criteria were neither random nor systematic, but based on the knowledge that certain institutions were successfully teaching science. Nor is my analysis of these exemplary programs "scientific." The objective has been simply to bring to life the places where good things are happening and the people who are making it so.

The heart of this volume is the case studies, detailed narratives of "programs that work." About a year in advance of the writing, an on-site *rapporteur* was employed to serve as the author's eyes and ears. Sometimes the rapporteur was a counselor, sometimes faculty, retired faculty, or faculty spouse, sometimes the department chair, but always someone with enough background to be able to report on the preselected program. The rapporteurs interviewed students, faculty, graduates, administrators, and other observers under my direction. They dug out the information needed to characterize the institution, describe the nature of the changes taking place, explain shifts in goals or activities and, above all, record how the participants interpreted events. At some point in the process the author made a site visit, sometimes more than one, to raise her own questions and to get a firsthand view.

Accordingly, the writing has been a collaborative process. The rapporteur provided a report from which the author composed an initial essay. This was circulated to the rapporteur and to the department or the course director for comments which were then integrated into later drafts. Eventually some kind of consensus emerged. This is not to say that everyone agrees with what is written here. But everyone has had an opportunity to elaborate on fragmentary reports, correct mistakes, and furnish additional background on themselves and on their work. A researcher exploring inertia and change in science education must be as interested in practitioners' views of their work as in the work itself, especially because successful reform is rare. Why should this be so?

The "Culture" of Science Education Reform

In contrast to actual success stories, science education reform at college tends to be consumed by the same "culture" of reform that has afflicted precollege science for decades. I use the term "culture" here the way it is defined by anthropologists David Schneider and Clifford Geertz, to refer to a group's shared meanings, its patterns of explanation and action, its intellectual *ecology*.[7] What is immediately striking about this "culture of reform" is how ardent and energetic reformers seem to

---

[7] Sharon Traweek, *Beamtimes and Lifetimes, The World of High Energy Physics* (Cambridge: Harvard University Press, 1988), p. 8.

be in inventing the new; yet how difficult reform is to implement, propagate, and sustain. They shake, but nothing moves.

Problem Hunting and Solution Finding

Trained in problem definition and problem solving, scientists inevitably bring the habits of doing science to the problem of reform. Thus, those who would reform science education often frame extremely complex issues in terms they are familiar with, namely, "problems" and "solutions." But reform is not a scientific enterprise. What problem hunting and problem solving may lead to instead is an oversimplification of extremely complex processes and a preference for theoretical, universal solutions over more modest, incremental change. Moreover, having identified one of these "solutions," scientist-reformers may not wish to compromise. Since their thinking is in terms of solutions rather than strategies, their recommendations are not expressed as options; nor are they rooted in the pragmatic, the real, the here and now. They do not offer people in the field (as one person I interviewed put it) any suggestions as to "what we can do tomorrow."

Another aspect of the science reform culture is that recommended changes are often out of context, both in terms of institutional limitations and the needs and abilities of the students and faculty they are supposed to serve. This indifference to context may also reflect the habits of doing science, for it appears to rest on an unexamined belief that, once articulated, the "right way" will be self-evident, teacher-proof, and appropriate for a wide variety of institutions. In the course of my research, I met so many scientist-science educators motivated by just such a vision that I constructed a composite *Weltanschauung*.

First, they believe there is one best curriculum or pedagogy waiting to be discovered, like the laws of nature, like quarks. If it hasn't been discovered so far, it's because researchers haven't worked hard enough. This idealized curriculum or pedagogy is not only "right," it is universal, and will work best irrespective of teacher, content, and place. Second, by pursuing abstract studies of the nature of knowledge and cognition, researchers can find this curriculum or pedagogy and experimentally prove it is the best. And third, such experimental evidence will persuade instructors everywhere to adopt the program.

Yet history proves that reforms adopted without reference to context are ill-fated. The much-heralded New Math delivered to the public schools in the 1960s and 1970s was—as later documented in a state-by-state study—not accompanied by sufficient investment in teacher retraining. As a result, implementation was spotty, which caused great difficulty (and much public outcry) when students moved. Mathematics educators also underestimated the need to reeducate parents at the same time they reeducated teachers. The result was, if not the "disaster" that mathematician Morris Kline spoke of,[8] certainly not the improvement which was intended.

The "grand reform" of college and precollege physics during the same period met with similar disappointment. In his history of physics curricular reform, 1955-1985, appropriately titled "Uses of the Past," physicist Arnold Arons summarizes decades of reform as having produced few innovations that have had lasting impact.[9] "Curricular devices and instructional formats have been invented and reinvented by succeeding generations," he writes, "and, in each reincarnation, are seized upon in the hope that a panacea has been found for instructional problems that fail to go away."

Arons' work is unusual in its attention to the past, and he chides the physics community for not reviewing the literature (the same criticism could be extended to education reformers more generally). "One traverses a steady stream of committee studies and reports," he writes, "which assess and reassess the same problems and make similar recommendations for improvement in almost identical phraseology without reference to the preceding reports and without inquiry into why so little change has taken place." This is not to say that nothing was achieved in the post-Sputnik era. The infusion of material resources and cultural support substantially strengthened the scientific community and contributed to scientific innovation. The problem is that educational reform in science and mathematics was neither mainstreamed nor sustained.[10]

Exclusive Emphasis on Materials and Delivery Systems

The great preponderance of efforts to reform science education has concentrated on course materials and teaching enhancements, what Arons calls "delivery systems." But this emphasis misses the mark. Recent experiments indicate that course materials and teaching enhancements are minor factors among those which make introductory college

---

[8] Morris Kline, *Why the Professor Can't Teach: Mathematics and the Dilemma of University Education* (New York: St. Martin's Press, 1977), p. 190.

[9] Arnold Arons, "Uses of the Past: Physics Curricular Reform 1955-1985," *Interchange*, Toronto, OISE, in press.

[10] Philip W. Jackson, "The Reform of Science Education: A Cautionary Tale," (1983) *Daedelus*, Vol. 112, No. 2, pp. 143-166. See also James Duderstadt's review of these matters in his keynote address as reprinted in *The Freshman Year in Science and Engineering*, Report of the Alliance for Undergraduate Education, 1991, p. 3.

science difficult to learn.[11] What hinders students are the pace, the conflicting purposes of the courses (to, variously, provide an introduction, or lay a foundation for a research career, or weed out the "unfit"); attitudes of their professors and fellow students; unexplained assumptions and conventions; exam design and grading practices; class size; the exclusive presentation of new material by means of lecture; and the absence of community–a host of variables that are not specifically addressed by most reforms.

This reluctance to grapple with the real issues has produced many failed reforms at the precollege level. Every teacher of science knows that the imaginative curriculum materials and hands-on kits produced by the 1960s Elementary Science Study (ESS), the Science Curriculum Improvement Study (SCIS), and Science, A Process Approach (SAPA), are now gathering dust in elementary school cloakrooms, some of them abandoned early on when there was no money to replace missing or damaged components, some never used because they were too difficult or time-consuming. Still, "materials development" remains the darling of precollege science reform, lately of college science reform as well. Why the nearly exclusive focus on instructional materials? Is it because these are products that give educational reformers and their paymasters something to show? Or is it that science education reformers, with some notable exceptions, don't know what else to do?

Innovation versus Managing Change

Innovation and change are presumed to operate in tandem. Innovation is considered, indeed, to be the *parent* of change. Yet in some instances (and science education reform is one of these) innovation and change are in competition for reformers' energies and dollars. In any such competition, innovation wins because innovation is more interesting than change–more experimental, less troublesome, and less political. But what if innovations have little effect on things as they are? No one wants to believe this, yet it may be true.

In their 1991 survey of projects to increase participation of minorities and women in college-level science, for example, Marsha Lakes Matyas and Shirley Malcom conclude that the programs installed in the 1980s were temporary and unconnected to other efforts on campus or off. These projects relied on short-term grants and, once these were exhausted, on

[11] Sheila Tobias, *They're Not Dumb, They're Different: Stalking the Second Tier* (Tucson, Ariz.: Research Corporation, 1990). See also Nancy M. Hewitt and Elaine Seymour, "Factors Contributing to High Attrition Rates Among Science, Mathematics, and Engineering Undergraduate Majors," (Report to the Alfred P. Sloan Foundation), Bureau of Sociological Research, Boulder, Colo., April 26, 1991.

volunteers.[12] Even where entire schools or departments were involved, projects addressed "only a small part of the overall system." What was missing, Matyas and Malcom make very explicit, was *structural reform*, substantial and permanent modification of existing courses, requirements, pedagogical techniques, recruitment, rewards; above all, change in institutional climate. Matyas and Malcom describe this failing quite baldly:[13]

> Most of the interventions devised by colleges and universities are aimed at enabling students and/or faculty from under-represented groups to fit into, adjust to, or negotiate the *existing system*. There is little challenge to the structures that currently exist. . . . The reconfiguration of the reward/incentive structure is seldom discussed as a means to achieve the appropriate balance. . . . In like manner, most existing efforts with students are designed to enable them to succeed in courses as they are *currently structured* [italics added].

Perhaps educators could learn something from industrial managers about what they call "innovation" but is actually managing change. Business has produced a large body of literature about change. Rosabeth Moss Kanter's *The Change Masters*, a much quoted study of innovative companies, documents again and again that innovation in large organizations (and physics departments or science divisions or school districts certainly qualify) requires "bargaining and negotiation" to get the information, support, and resources needed for change.[14] Corporate managers call this process "buying-in," meaning that the innovator must estimate the proper level of effort needed and "presell" the idea by getting key individuals involved. In short, the innovator must work as hard on peer support as on designing the innovation itself. None of this, needless to say, is achieved when the innovator insists on working alone and then tries to foist the innovation on the system from without. Above all, reform requires flexibility. "A working compromise," the change masters believe, "is better than an optimal solution, poorly implemented."

The process of transforming innovation into change—even getting teachers to accept the findings of educational research[15]—is essentially

---

[12] Matyas and Malcom, *Investing in Human Potential . . .*, p. 144.

[13] Matyas and Malcom, *Investing in Human Potential . . .*, p. 130.

[14] Rosabeth Moss Kanter, *The Change Masters* (New York: Simon and Schuster, 1983).

[15] Virginia Richardson, "Significant and Worthwhile Change in Teaching Practice," *Educational Researcher*, October 1990, pp. 10-17.

political. And it is necessary to ask political questions: Who wants change? Who is going to be made to feel insecure? Who profits from the status quo? How can the necessary players be gathered to counter institutional inertia? And, most important, how can the innovation be structured, even if this means it is less "perfect," so that it serves other needs of the organization? Many educational reformers, scientists in particular, fail to understand how *political* this process is and, even when they do, don't have the diplomatic skills (or the stomach) to see it through.

The "Burden" of Intermittent Funding

Another factor in the failure of innovative reforms to produce permanent change is the presumption that anything new and good has to be funded from the outside. What actually happens is very often the reverse of what was intended. A faculty member suggesting any improvement, even a modest one, is likely to be told by the department chair that outside funding will be a prerequisite. But an outside agency is not interested in backing a modest improvement, only an "innovation" that has a distinctive ring. To get funding, then, the reform-minded faculty member refashions a modest improvement into an overblown innovation complete with plans for evaluation and dissemination. With a little luck it will get support, but when funding runs out, the innovator moves on to another project, or the outcome (by some measure) is less than significant and the funders lose patience, the reform dies a premature death. Worse yet are the messages conveyed: reform is a dubious undertaking; reformers are required to get their own money; standard programs have first dibs on mainstream funds.

Turning a good idea into something that can be funded means that a very complex issue may be oversimplified and local problems of implementation ignored. As one example, a physics department committee in a large state university correctly determined that beefing up their woefully underused physics education major would require creative marketing on the one hand, and hard-nosed negotiation to reduce requirements in *both* physics and education on the other. There was nothing in these necessary negotiations that would appeal to an outside funding agency. So the committee members decided instead to do what they *enjoyed* doing, namely, designing a new teacher-education course in physics. Not a bad idea in itself, but they shied away from the harder political battle and proposed something that might garner outside support.

So familiar is the grants writing process that in some universities "instructional improvement" is commensurate with doling out internal funds to internal applicants for short-term projects, including new course development. The doling out committee thus spends its time reviewing applications to experiment instead of tackling the infrastructural barriers to real change.

Apart from the burden on innovators of writing proposals and the postponement of difficult political struggles that are inevitable if mainstream privileges and resources are going to be redirected, innovation through outside funding has other disadvantages. Funding for individual projects is inevitably short-term and intermittent–exactly what is counterindicated for long-term change. So even though such proposals include plans to evaluate and to disseminate, innovations tend to disappear when either the innovator moves on to another project or the funding cycle ends–as one department chairman told me bluntly, "When our funding stops, we're dead." Money has been wrongly perceived to be the *prime mover* of change.

Another Model: Cumulative Improvement

In his article "A Nation At Risk, Revisited," written three years after *A Nation at Risk* was published, Gerald Holton makes the point that what we need is not more short-term programs, but "a device that encourages cumulative improvement over the long haul," a strategy that, at its core, involves close attention to things as they are and, in place of one-shot cure-alls, a commitment to ongoing change.[16] Unlike universal solutions produced by outside experts or innovations in the hands of creative loners, cumulative improvement challenges on-line managers (professors, department chairs, and deans) to determine what is possible in the near or midterm.

A number of science education reformers seem to be doing something like this, combining innovation and management of change, although they use somewhat different terms. The cases that follow illustrate this approach: the improvement is specific, the constituency defined, and institutionalization is given high priority. While the jury is still out on how well these reforms achieve long-range objectives, they are all doable, high-leverage activities that appear among the most promising.

Strategies Versus Solutions

My conclusion is that the search for a panacea for the problems of teaching and learning undergraduate science will inevitably be disappointing. The reason reform is sought by means of instructional materials

---

[16] Gerald Holton, "A Nation at Risk, Revisited," *The Advancement of Science and its Burdens* (Cambridge, England: The Press Syndicate of the University of Cambridge, 1986), p. 277.

and teaching enhancements is not that anyone really expects a perfect course or pedagogy to be devised, but because we are accustomed to doing reform in this manner. The temptation is to solve a problem with a product (or, in the case of the Matyas-Malcom survey, a project) because for innovators and funders alike, the alternatives are harder to conceptualize. If there is no single universal solution, and if an experimental model does not lead the way to it, what are we to do?

The one answer college administrators fear most is that whatever we do it will be harder, of longer duration, more ambitious, and overall more difficult politically and psychologically to sustain than a relatively straightforward short-term experiment. This does not mean that some increase in our knowledge base is not useful, but it does mean we cannot expect change to occur either as an automatic result of increased knowledge, or as an outcome of almost randomly generated innovation. To rely on short-term experiments is to misunderstand the educational process and, ultimately, to mismanage its reform.

The history of science education reform is littered with well-intentioned failures. What is to guarantee that even programs that work today will still be around and still be working tomorrow?

2

High Morale in a Stable Environment
Chemistry at UW-Eau Claire

A group of ten University of Wisconsin-Eau Claire chemistry students is having lunch with me. I met four of them earlier on a tour of the chemistry laboratories where they were participating in faculty research. We are discussing the process by which they came to chemistry, what they expect of Eau Claire, and why they are enthusiastic about science as a career. As they talk about themselves and their backgrounds, the sociologist in me notes that they don't fit the model of precommitted ("first tier") students of science. With one or two exceptions, they came to chemistry late and find it satisfying but *hard*.

Two of the ten failed chemistry at least once on the way to becoming chemistry majors, one in high school, one at college. It was only the latter student's willingness to leave school for a while in order to mature, and the department's readiness to take him back by way of chem 099, a kind of make-up course for those who didn't take chemistry in high school, that provided him with a second chance. Three of the ten came to college planning to major in the biological sciences or premed. They took chemistry the first time because they had to, but were soon recruited to the major. One who "hated" chemistry until her junior year in high school is doing extremely well in Eau Claire's innovative chemistry with business emphasis program (locally, "chem-biz").

None of my lunchmates is the offspring of a scientist. Like most at Eau Claire (43 percent are from west central Wisconsin including Eau Claire and the seventeen surrounding rural counties), the majority are first-generation college-goers, so this is not surprising. But the ability of the Eau Claire chemistry department to attract first-generation college students to science is impressive, particularly in the face of statistical evidence that shows that even scientists' children eschew science.

The students in my lunch group like the personal attention they get from their professors, the "open door" policy–students are welcome to drop in anytime and chat about their work–and that they get their homework back on time, and carefully graded. Despite medium class size (forty to sixty at the upper levels, seventy-five to eighty in the freshman course), professors know students by name early in the semester. Part of the reason is that the introductory course involves a four-hour lab every week taught by the professor. This means that the faculty member responsible for the freshman course sees eighty students in three one-hour classes per week and one-third of the class at a time in three four-hour labs.

Collaborative Research

For the students I am meeting, the research lab is a key attraction of the chemistry major. As at other institutions with established undergraduate research programs, it is a "different kind of experience" from class, they tell me, providing hands-on science and a place where they can work with both their professors and classmates. When I wandered with them to their lab stations earlier that morning, I was struck by their understanding of the research they were doing and by their ability to explain it to me, a nonchemist. One student, for example, is making an organic compound *no one has ever made before* (his emphasis). Certain proteins, he explains, have a soft metal such as copper at their center. He and his professor, Leo Ochrymowycz, one of the first faculty members at Eau Claire to implement a regular program of scholarly research with students, are working to get the sulfurs to "point in" in the rings. In that process, the student is discovering that there is "beauty" (his word) in the compounds he is creating. Few people work in this area, he assures me, which makes it all the more exciting.

Another student, working with Scott Hartsel, professor of biochemistry, is developing a new technique for measuring "transmembrane ion currents caused by amphotericin B." (I notice that she doesn't stumble on any of this nomenclature.) The antibiotic is known to attack systemic fungal infections in immune-suppressed patients. It could have applications in treating AIDS, leukemia, and transplant patients, but some have bad side effects from the drug. Her work might contribute toward a more efficacious variant of the antibiotic, which gets her excited about her research. She works ten hours a week for a combination of pay and independent study credit. Even though she deals with substances she has not yet studied in biochemistry class (such as lipids, she says to me), she finds that she understands the topic when it finally comes up in her course. She doesn't know it at the time we talk, but she will be the only undergraduate presenting a poster session on her work at the Biophysical Society Meeting in the spring of 1991, and is headed for graduate school in biochemistry at University of Wisconsin-Madison.

Around the corner in the physical chemistry ("p-chem") lab, another young woman is working at the macroscopic level with physical chemist Al Denio on a project involving recyclable materials such as plastic, tin, and glass. One use for pellets made from these materials would be to replace sand and asphalt-eroding salt currently strewn on Wisconsin's winter roads to melt ice. But before the pellets can be recommended as a salt substitute the lab team will study how ice structure can be modified, the effects on tires of any single material and various combinations, and what their effects would be on asphalt. The student is actually grinding up materials and cutting them into pellets as I watch. Like the other undergraduates, she understands the "bigger picture" as it applies to her project and appears very comfortable talking chemistry.

Student-faculty collaborative research is an important component of the chemistry major at UW-Eau Claire. Many undergraduate schools require a senior project for graduation, but at Eau Claire it is up to the student and an individual faculty member to plan such an undertaking. While the specific project will be defined by the faculty member, students participate in the initial literature search, plan and execute experiments, and do a preliminary analysis of the results. Students may do laboratory work for faculty members any time after completing the general chemistry sequence, often as early as the sophomore year. Undergraduates are paid, some through work-study funds and others from the faculty member's own grants. With no chemistry graduate students at Eau Claire, all laboratory places go to undergraduates, but there is still plenty of competition. Not all students who do collaborative research are from the chemistry department. Faculty member Fred King, a theoretical chemist, often uses students from physics, math, and computer science to work on large (up to several hundred hours on the supercomputer) theoretical problems. Research is a very popular activity.

Because students can work on a project for several consecutive years, their experience is cumulative. By junior or senior year many are presenting poster sessions or papers at conferences. Not surprisingly, students who do collaborative research with faculty attend graduate school at a higher rate (about 75 percent) than those who do not (55 percent). As the faculty views it, it is in their laboratories that students learn *for themselves* that science is interesting and that they can have some "ownership" of the subject. And because they are working on "real-world" projects, they gain firsthand knowledge of the scientific process. Faculty find that in the one-on-one setting they can encourage their young research collaborators to pursue careers in science.

A senior interviewed for this report comments that his collaborative research experience and his published papers are giving him the equivalent experience of a first- or second-year graduate student. "Besides," he adds, "doing research breaks up the routine of classwork. . . . It allows me to work together with my professor to get things done, not in the traditional professor-student relationship, but as peers." A junior working with Jack Pladziewicz notes that "classwork in chemistry is very structured, everything set out in advance." Working in the lab she finds herself dealing with problems that are not "predefined," problems "no one has yet been able to answer. It is more challenging, requiring more focus and causing us to think through our results." Another student particularly appreciates getting a foretaste of the poster sessions and papers she will give as a professional. "As a scientist, I'll have to do this during my whole career."

Why Eau Claire is Different

In a typical large state university 3,000 or more undergraduates enroll in general chemistry each year, of which only about thirty will end up as majors. To be sure, most of the 3,000 initially have no intention of majoring in science. They are taking chemistry to fulfill prerequisites in other fields or to satisfy their "science requirement" for graduation. But in the pool are students who could be wooed into science. Smaller state universities and the independent colleges manage to attract and retain about the same number of majors per year from much smaller pools of freshman enrollees. How do they do this? What can we learn from their programs? And can what we learn be implemented elsewhere?

Since the first chemistry degree was earned at UW-Eau Claire in 1957, more than 500 students have completed the traditional chemistry major. Approximately 55 percent of these majors have done advanced work in graduate, medical, or other professional schools, with ninety-two students attaining the Ph.D. degree, 102 the M.S. degree, and more than eighty obtaining degrees in medicine, dentistry, and veterinary medicine. Nearly thirty became high school teachers and many more are currently making progress toward advanced degrees. An additional 200 students earned degrees in chem-biz since the start of this program in 1973. More than 90 percent of these majors are employed in technical positions.

"We believe that the success of our graduates is a positive indicator of both the quality of our students and of our program."[1] So begins a chemistry department development proposal, which reflects both the department's impressive production of graduates and its willingness to share credit for success with the students it recruits. It doesn't take long

---

[1]Department development proposal, February 1991

for an outsider to discover that this sharing of credit is a hallmark of the chemistry department. The faculty is even more unusual in that it has (1) a collective commitment to make the program work; (2) an absence of political infighting, and instead, real, palpable affection among members (Jack Pladziewicz refers to the department as a "familial, harmonious non-fiefdom"); and (3) faculty members who are *where they want to be*.[2] One of the newer faculty members, Scott Hartsel, was considering a position at an eastern university while looking over Eau Claire. He chose Eau Claire because "the students are good, hard-working kids who don't take their education for granted." Another new faculty member, Warren Gallagher, believes Eau Claire to be a "great environment." "I want to teach and I want to do research," he says. "Eau Claire provides the opportunity to do both."

In 1990-1991 there were forty-five declared chemistry majors at UW-Eau Claire, as well as twenty-seven majoring in chem-biz, thirteen in chemistry education, and forty-one in biochemistry-molecular biology (a major considered to be interdisciplinary with biology). Of UW-Eau Claire's twenty-five or so graduating seniors, about 60 percent will work for a faculty member during their years in the major. There are work opportunities for students: of the seventeen faculty members in chemistry (one is chancellor of the university), ten enjoy outside funding for research in which undergraduates can participate.

There is nothing unusual about the general chemistry curriculum at UW-Eau Claire, I am assured. "If you're looking for innovation," Jack Pladziewicz told me on my arrival in the fall of 1990, "you've come to the wrong place." In their minds, the faculty aren't doing anything *new* (except perhaps for the major in chem-biz); rather, they are doing things *well*. Indeed, the course structure and sequence appear to an outsider to be standard. While the chemistry majors seem to the department (and to me) to be very satisfied with their curriculum, the department is committed to improvement. One focus of attention is the two five-credit courses in the introductory sequence, chem 103-104. The department is very aware that chem 103-104 students are not necessarily chemistry majors (usually found in a different sequence), and that only some will be recruited to chemistry. Still, the department takes seriously its responsibility to the 474 students enrolled, as it does to the 120 prenursing students enrolled in chem 152. Most faculty members take a turn teaching this introductory sequence, so every faculty member is familiar with the needs of students that these courses attract.

---

[2] In what follows, the interviews conducted by rapporteur Stella Pagonis provide an important corroboration to my own impressions.

Not all the professors at Eau Claire are gifted teachers. But recently retired department chair Mel Gleiter assures me that "the program is so good that poor teaching doesn't have the negative consequences it would have in another place." Still, continuous (even compulsive) improvement seems to be the rule. Even though first-year chem 103 and 104 are successfully recruiting new majors, the department is moving toward some restructuring. The intention is to have chem 103 deal with "issues" and to structure the standard topics in chemistry around these issues. The rationale, one faculty member tells me, is to show students "how empowering a knowledge of chemistry can be."

A curriculum committee, known locally as G-C 3 (General Chemistry Curriculum Committee), was recently revived after several years of dormancy. The goals of G-C 3 are modest, says Judy Lund, one of its members, and are "to improve the general chemistry courses because there is a common perception that they need to be improved." No grand schemes here, and no certainty that the faculty will readily agree on how. The revival of G-C 3 simply gives an already committed faculty an opportunity to talk a little more systematically about the entry level curriculum. The fact that new faculty are expected to sit in on these deliberations conveys to them early on how important teaching and thinking about teaching are to this department.

Dedication to Teaching

Many of the students who are recruited to chemistry at UW-Eau Claire are "nontraditional." They are not primed for science, and indeed, their backgrounds may be weak or incomplete. Such students have not yet learned how to "teach themselves," hence teaching in the broadest sense of providing both guidance and welcome is of critical importance in recruiting, retaining, and launching these students in science. This does not mean chemistry is in any way "watered down." During my visit, I sit in on a fast-paced general course for students intending to major in the sciences. While listening to the lecturer treat atomic structure and quantum theory (including a discussion of the logic behind Schroedinger's equation), I assume this is an advanced class. But in fact the students are newcomers to the material.

Forty-five students are enrolled in this class, about half of them female. I learn later that chemistry's ability to attract and retain female majors is one of its many strong points. The School of Arts and Sciences enrolls about 4,470 students of whom 58 percent are female. Of the 126 students majoring in chemistry or in chemistry-related fields, 59 percent are male and 41 percent female, almost exactly the inverse in gender, but a very good record compared to other undergraduate institutions. Considering that about 58 percent of the chemistry majors (excluding chem-biz) who graduated from UW-Eau Claire have gone on to graduate or professional schools (519 since 1957 when the major was first offered), the department qualifies as an important feeder school for graduate chemists in general and women graduate chemists in particular. Recruitment, and above all *retention*, of female faculty members through the tenure process is a newer priority.

Bob Eierman, professor in the class I chose to audit, is an unabashed devotee of some of the newest theory and practice in science pedagogy. He gives the class a handout listing goals and objectives for each unit and employs an interactive style. In addition to questioning students and calling on them individually by name, the professor has them do exercises, short problems worked on together. He calls them "Whimbey pairs" after Art Whimbey, a researcher in problem solving. Eierman also regularly interrupts his own lecture to ask students to "explain this idea to your neighbor." But at least as important as pedagogy, he tells me, is having fewer than 100 students in a science class. "Once you say 'yes' to the large class, you've said 'no' to all manner of teaching," he says emphatically.

Recruiting Faculty and Students

That the department is dedicated to teaching is obvious in the care with which classes are assigned, the accessibility of faculty, the real research opportunities provided majors, and the commitment to continuous improvement as evidenced by revival of G-C 3. Another important factor is how interest in and aptitude for teaching influences the hiring process. Mark Krahling, one of three assistant professors recently hired, was encouraged to talk about his high school teaching (prior to graduate school) during his job interview. Warren Gallagher was specifically asked about his commitment to teaching when he interviewed for his position.

The department understands that to maintain a full complement of majors it has not only to retain students, but recruit from west central Wisconsin high schools. Judy Lund and Eau Claire undergraduates take chemistry demo shows to elementary schools to stir early interest, and Mark Krahling recruits UW-Eau Claire faculty to visit local high schools. A more ambitious project is to build a mobile chemistry demonstration unit and take it to high schools throughout the region. Such a unit, to be staffed by chemistry majors, was in the planning stages when this was written. Other means of promoting university to high school partnerships are on the new vice chancellor's agenda.

Placement

At the other end of the recruitment pipeline is placement, more formalized in chemistry at UW-Eau Claire than in other departments or at most other nonengineering undergraduate institutions. Faculty member Leo Ochrymowycz has assigned himself the task of placing graduates and has become a specialist in locating jobs in pure and industrial chemistry. But he does not work alone. Every faculty member does individual counseling and postgraduate mentoring, and two other members systematically maintain industrial contacts.

The process begins in the middle of the junior year when chemistry majors are invited to talk about their future plans. "Chemists aren't free-lancers," Ochrymowycz explains to me as he does to the students who come to him for guidance. "Chemists need the resources only employers can provide. We can have more autonomy within a megacorporation than most other employees, but we are still employees." Successfully placed alumni help to extend the reach of the professor. One employer (Vista Chemical) in far away Houston, Texas, has recruited nine chem and chem-biz majors from UW-Eau Claire in the past decade, usually taking one per graduating class. The connection was made through the first student placed, who is still with the company. In gratitude, and with an eye toward recruiting more graduates, the company recently established a chem-biz scholarship fund.

Interdisciplinary Programs in Chemistry

Chem-biz was introduced at UW-Eau Claire in 1973, and is the only program of its type in the Midwest and one of a very few in the country. There have been 224 graduates, of whom over 90 percent have been placed in industrial companies. Phil Chenier, student adviser and author of a textbook on industrial chemistry, tells me that chem-biz students compete successfully both with business majors because of their affinity for technical subjects, and with chemical engineers because of their business training. The major requires thirty-three credit hours in chemistry (including applied physical chemistry in place of standard p-chem); a course in industrial chemistry; and thirty credit hours in the school of business. In 1990-91, there were twenty-seven students (thirteen male, fourteen female) enrolled in the major.

Clearly, there is a market for these graduates, and it is surprising that the business department is not as enthusiastic about chem-biz as chemistry. Perhaps it is because chem-biz students consider themselves in chemistry; their advisers, their internships, and their placement are through the department. One student interviewed admitted to feeling like an outsider in business. She told me, and most likely conveyed this impression to her business professors as well, that her business courses were boring and nonchallenging in comparison to chemistry.

During their senior year chem-biz majors attend a spring seminar sponsored by the Department of Chemistry at which industrial representatives are invited to talk about their own jobs and about the wide variety of opportunities that the chem-biz combination has to offer. Last spring seminar speakers included a marketing manager from a salt company, a sales representative from a pharmaceutical firm, and an industrial scientist looking for alternate uses of industrial waste. Positions offered seniors included one in supply and transportation for a chemical company, sales in plastics, and process control in paper manufacturing. Chem-biz students are very positive about chemistry.

Teacher Preparation

Chemistry teaching is the curriculum designed for students aiming to become high school chemistry teachers. There is a marked need for them in Wisconsin and elsewhere, and it is a career for which many UW-Eau Claire students with a bent for science are primed. While local educators believe the curriculum provides an excellent, well-rounded education for prospective teachers, it is prohibitively long and involved, requiring a complete major in chemistry (thirty-six credit hours, including p-chem), a minor (twenty-four credit hours) in biology, math, or physics, a chemistry department requirement of math and physics (twenty-two credit hours), and a professional sequence in secondary education (forty-four credit hours). To satisfy the Wisconsin State Department of Public Instruction, this coursework must be separate and distinct from the university's requirement of forty-three credit hours of general education. Therefore, to graduate with a chemistry teaching major, a student needs between 160 and 169 credit hours, compared to 128 for most other majors and 147 for other education students. A student has to be dedicated to teaching to acquire an additional thirty-two credits–about one academic year. And it is especially discouraging to receive only a teacher's entry level salary after five years of study, especially when chemistry and chem-biz graduates command much more. Most students are not so dedicated. There have been only thirty graduates in chemistry teaching since the major began in 1957, just four in 1989-1992. As a fifth-year student currently doing her student teaching stated, "three of us in one year is extremely rare!"

Resistance to changing the requirements comes from all sides. The Wisconsin State Department of Public Instruction requires all education students to take certain subjects. The chemistry department wants prospective chemistry teachers to obtain a regular degree in chemistry. Another complication is that students of science find their education courses to be nonrigorous ("insipid" was the term used by one student). The kind of material covered, and the performance demanded by these courses are, one might say, culturally estranging for students of science. Worse yet, majors in chemistry teaching do not have room in their schedules for such important chemistry electives as biochemistry, inorganic chemistry, and instrumental analysis.

Education requirements are rigid. One student who had been tutoring children in the nearby Hmong community (a neighborhood of Laotian refugees who settled in large numbers in Eau Claire[3]) was not able to count this experience toward her education foundations requirement dealing with teaching minorities. The chemistry department seems unable to effect any changes in this critical teaching major. The problem is not its interdisciplinary character, because biochemistry-molecular biology–a joint program between the Departments of Chemistry and Biology established in 1988–is doing well. In 1990-1991, chem teaching had thirteen declared majors and biochemistry-molecular biology had forty-one. The problem, according to Dean Nelson (not a dean, but a member of the chemistry department who advises chem ed majors) is the all but required fifth year.

The Two Interdisciplinary Majors Compared

It is instructive to compare the low student enrollment in chemistry teaching with the popularity of biochemistry-molecular biology. One thing that struck me as an outsider is the absence from the chemistry faculty of anyone with a formal background in chemistry education. Dean Nelson, who enjoys recruiting students to the chemistry teaching major and encourages them along the way, is himself a 1958 graduate of Eau Claire's chemistry teaching program. But there is no one in the department–and this is my view, not theirs–who could (as an insider) negotiate a compromise curriculum with faculty in the School of Education. Many of the chemistry faculty, notably the current chairman Joel Klink, are deeply interested in chem ed at the college level. But theirs is an informal, praxis-oriented expertise, not grounded in a studied, theoretical perspective. So, after the 1977 retirement of the one chemistry education specialist (a senior woman hired in 1946 when UW-Eau Claire was Eau Claire Normal School), there has only been one chemistry education doctorate employed.

[3]Thao Yang, perhaps the only Hmong Ph.D. biochemist in the country, was appointed to the UW-Eau Claire chemistry department in 1991.

Another difference is in the two curricula themselves. Molecular biology and biochemistry are relatively new and exciting areas of science. Thus it was not difficult for chemistry to persuade itself that it was in its own interest, as well as that of its students, to launch a new interdisciplinary major. Faculty recruitment has been steady and successful. Of the last five hires in chemistry, three (Scott Hartsel, Warren Gallagher, and Thao Yang) are in biochemistry. Hartsel and Gallagher spoke enthusiastically about their freedom to create a new curriculum. "There are no rules, no history. We get to design the courses and devise the labs," said Gallagher. As a result, the new major is "sucking students into the department," mostly from biology.

But a third factor, surely, is the School of Education's unwillingness to reduce its own requirements and to pressure other departments into initiating courses geared to education majors. In the absence of dedicated financial aid for prospective science teachers, which would free some Eau Claire students from having to work while in school, a 160-credit-hour major requiring a fifth year of undergraduate education is not a way to advertise either the discipline or careers in chemistry teaching.

Analysis

What makes the chemistry program at UW-Eau Claire work? Why, in a period of declining enrollments in the chemistry major around the country, do 126 undergraduates choose to major in chemistry or in one of the chemistry-related fields at Eau Claire when (on average) many research-oriented state universities with three or four times the student body can boast only half that number? And what is the likelihood that the department can retain its high morale and recruitment success in a period of more stringent budgets? The answers suggested here grow from data provided by the department, a site visit by myself, and several months of interviewing by Stella Pagonis, my on-site rapporteur.

The factors that contribute to successful recruitment and retention of students in chemistry at Eau Claire are found at other colleges and universities that focus attention on their undergraduates. The chemistry departments at Eau Claire, Fort Lewis College, and Trinity University (see chapter 3) all have recruited faculty over the years who consider themselves to be dedicated teachers, as well as active in research, and on all three campuses faculty and student collaborative research is an essential component of the major.

Sociological variables are not to be overlooked. At many comprehensive state universities the majority of the faculty are, if not first-generation college-goers, certainly first-generation college faculty. At UW-Eau

Claire, of the eighteen faculty in chemistry (including the chancellor), twelve grew up on farms or come from small towns, two are from Eau Claire itself, and thirteen are, in fact, the first of their families to attend college. Although the faculty finds its students to be of "widely varying ability and preparation" and often intellectually "immature," there is little indication of a class gap between faculty and students. And although all tenured members of the department are white and male, there is no "gender gap" as far as recruitment of female students is concerned, a tribute to the department's determination not to turn anyone away.

At the time I began studying the department, there were no tenurable women in the department and the lack of female faculty was an admitted embarrassment. But two women have recently been appointed to tenure-track positions. Even before the new appointments, faculty members were determined to rectify the imbalance because they believed that "a woman with a regular appointment is important as a role model to female students." UW-Eau Claire has a recently appointed female vice chancellor, Marjorie Smeltsor, who encourages female hires to prove "you don't have to be white and male to do chemistry."

Still, tenure decisions are difficult to make. Student opinion is not always a significant factor even in a department as committed as this one to excellence in teaching. The department recently denied tenure to a professor who had extremely strong letters of student support, justifying the decision on the grounds that, in terms of research potential and productivity, "the department felt it could do better." But how much better can the department do in a competition for research-oriented chemists when it demands a teaching load of twelve to sixteen contact hours and 260 student credit hours per faculty per semester?

As in most comprehensive state universities the problem is that the university demands scholarly (research) activity, but ties the number of faculty positions to student credit hours. Although the department tries to balance teaching and scholarship, it is limited in its power to reward good teaching with tenure or to reduce credit hours to support efforts to improve. As one example of how the credit hour issue confounds pedagogy, consider collaborative research, so important to teaching and student satisfaction with the chemistry major at Eau Claire, yet not counted toward teaching time.

A recent internal audit of the department resulted in a recommendation that the department make collaborative research a requirement for the chemistry major so that time spent with students could be counted as teaching time. This would reduce the number of course contact hours for faculty, a welcome relief from the sixteen hours required. But department philosophy got in the way: not every student wants to do collaborative research, the department believes, and not every student should. If collaborative research were to become a requirement, it could become a burden for students and instructors alike. In any case the department believes it ought to decide what is required for the major and what is not, credit-hour formulas notwithstanding. The new vice-chancellor agrees. Her policy is to allocate personnel on the basis of a department's accomplishments, not merely on the basis of its load.

A related concern is faculty overload, particularly for younger members. To obtain tenure a new faculty member must teach and advise; write grant applications to get funding for research, equipment, and summer salaries; do scholarly research and present or publish the findings; and serve on departmental and university committees. Participation in civic affairs is also expected. This puts enormous pressure, as the internal audit stated, on probationary members to establish their research credentials at the same time they are attempting to teach the department's courses. And teaching, however masterful and effective in shaping and reshaping the department's program, is not always counted as scholarship. Echoing Ernest Boyer,[4] Chairman Joel Klink wants to encourage scholarly activity in *either* research or pedagogy, but how many of his colleagues outside of Eau Claire would do the same? The constraints described above are not unique to UW-Eau Claire. The question is whether chemistry's very special commitment to teaching and its tradition of steady if undramatic improvement can be sustained in an indifferent larger world which emphasizes breakthroughs with economic potential.

Conclusion: High Morale in a Stable Environment

A major contribution to high morale in UW-Eau Claire's chemistry department is the general consensus as to the role of chemistry within the university. The department sees itself as having three jobs: first, to graduate chemistry majors; second, to accommodate students who have to take chemistry; and third, to introduce the concepts of chemistry to general students and show how it relates to their everyday lives. This consensus is reflected in the number of students majoring in chemistry, the large percentage who go on to graduate school, and the attention paid to finding ways to improve the already high quality of instruction in chemistry—and not just for majors. The replacement of chem 099 with a new tandem course in chemistry and general skills can serve as one example of how the process of continuous improvement works locally and at little cost.

---

[4] See Ernest L. Boyer, *Scholarship Reconsidered: Priorities of the Professoriate* (Princeton, N.J.: Carnegie Foundation for the Advancement of Teaching, 1990), chap. 1.

Until this year, students not yet ready for general chemistry (primarily nursing students and unsuccessful first-year students) were invited to take chemistry 099 (preparatory chemistry), usually offered in the fall, and chemistry 103 in the spring. But since the next course in the sequence for nurses, chemistry 152 (survey of biochemistry), was offered only in the spring, a student nurse who enrolled in chemistry 099 would fall one whole year behind. Faculty member Ralph Marking saw this as a problem and began to look for alternatives. The availability of an academic skills center on campus, willing and able to offer remedial sections for courses in sociology, psychology, and economics, gave him an idea which he implemented in fall 1991. Today, students not ready for chem 103 are encouraged to register for the course and lab for five credit hours and simultaneously enroll in a study skills course called "introduction to studying the sciences" (gen 101) for four additional credit hours. So while chem 099 is still in the catalog, its constituents are now doing the new tandem sequence.

And so far the supplementary coursework is producing good results. Those who took gen 101 in fall 1991 had a higher average grade point in chem 103 than the standard students, and the percentage of gen 101 students proceeding to chem 152 or chem 104 is the same as the standard student rate of 40 to 50 percent. Furthermore, 75 percent of the gen 101 students are taking a science and/or math course in spring 1992, certainly a good showing.

What's interesting, apart from the pedagogical advantage of having beginning students immersed in chemistry for a total of nine (out of a possible twelve or fifteen) credit hours, is the way the improvement was managed. An individual faculty member, hearing from students about their scheduling problems, undertook to find a solution, gathered support and assistance from the academic skills staff, and applied to the UW system for modest start-up funds. The grant was awarded and the new program is now in place. Whether gen 101 succeeds will depend, of course, on how well the students do in succeeding chemistry classes. The advantage of this low-cost local initiative is obvious. It's tailor-made for the needs of the students at hand. But its rapid implementation might not have been possible in a department that did not actively encourage its faculty to take the initiative.

"In a corporate environment," says Pagonis (whose training is in management), "the overall attitude of a department is a reflection of its management." In this case, leadership is not uniquely located in the office of the chair. Rather, department leadership is shared among the most respected faculty, which may and often does include the chair. As leaders, however, these senior faculty tend to downplay their authority.

They lead not by intimidation, but rather by example, suggestion, and recommendation. They work hard and expect the same from their junior faculty. They communicate openly and are mutually admiring. One hears: "Leo is tireless in his placement efforts," or "Fred is the shining star in publishing and obtaining grant money," or "The biochemistry program is in very capable hands."

The internal audit referred to previously noted that "the expectations of the department exceed what any one person could reasonably handle." But the problem of faculty burnout was never verbalized in any of our interviews. Some faculty members had complaints: lack of standardized testing, lack of space to store demonstrations, insensitivity of the administration–things that are important to them; but no one believed any of these factors affected their overall performance. In chemistry, there is an effort to achieve (to use Pladziewicz's language) a kind of "common good." And the students respond both to the better-than-average-teaching that is the hallmark of the department, and to its commitment to career placement, something that other faculty in the liberal arts rarely attend to or even consider to be part of their jobs.

Success feeds on itself. Alumni constitute one set of disciples, spreading the good word. Faculty members at other Wisconsin campuses are another, regularly recommending UW-Eau Claire for its chemistry program. Department members truly believe that theirs is a stellar program and that by doing a good job in challenging students, they can and do draw the best and the most motivated to chemistry. This is a remarkable achievement for a public university with students of varied ability, background, and social status and, given the elitism that characterizes science elsewhere, it results from an even more remarkable point of view.

3

Recruiting New Students to Research Science
Fort Lewis and Trinity

Fort Lewis College in Durango, Colorado and Trinity University in San Antonio, Texas are about as far away, geographically and ethnically, from UW-Eau Claire as Eau Claire is from Cal State LA (see chapter 9). What these four institutions have in common are chemistry programs that "work," and not because of a revolutionary new curriculum or pedagogy or external funding (although Cal State LA does benefit from outside support). Even a cursory examination of their programs reveals the significance of factors the nation can no more "purchase" than impose. Nothing to invent, nothing to discover, nothing to manufacture, nothing to import. What succeeds is obvious to anyone who looks at a program that works.

First, there is commitment, not just to teaching, but to students, young people who are taking, for whatever reason, one or more courses in science. The faculty at these institutions *care* about their students personally and not just about their work in chemistry. Indeed, the key to success in recruiting and retaining traditional and nontraditional students in science resides–beyond doubt, it seems to me–in the warm fuzzies these departments provide, along with excellence in teaching, opportunities for research, and a marked absence of elitism.

"I am pleased you contacted me about my undergraduate experience at Fort Lewis," writes a student now in a Ph.D. program at the University of Nevada, Reno. "Dr. Ritchey took special interest in my education. . . . His enthusiasm and his extra help gave me success in my first chemistry course, and he remained my mentor for my years at Fort Lewis." By second semester, he was "beginning to view chemistry with real interest, not just as a means to an end." The department offered a study room in which chem majors would "hang out." "It was here," the student writes, "that my feeling solidified that chemistry was something special." By the third semester he was "hooked on a chemistry major."

Today Fort Lewis graduates as many chemistry majors per year (currently sixteen out of a total student body of 4,000) as do many of the large state universities with enrollments of six to seven times as many students.

What about the common factors at successful institutions? Departmental politics, structure, and morale are among them. In each of the institutions where chemistry programs appear to be working, decisions are made by democratic process, even, as at UW-Eau Claire and Fort Lewis, by consensus. In departments where chairs rotate and/or are elected, responsibility for programs as well as hiring is shared. The importance of morale cannot be overemphasized. Critical decisions that affect teaching and class size are made by the department and these decisions make and unmake students' choices about majoring in the discipline. Teaching assignments are second only to hiring policy in determining the quality of instruction.

These departments know that the assignment of a poor lecturer to a freshman or sophomore course (because that faculty member is not doing research or is being punished for some reason) can "unmake" dozens of prospective majors.

A concern and a reverence for teaching pervades departments where programs work. Every faculty member feels responsible if any course (and not just their own) is not going well. Faculty members take turns in study rooms. Their doors are open to students having trouble. Where departments are small, course problems get immediate attention, "no longer than one day" after being reported, says the Fort Lewis chairman. Where departments are large, the faculty construct mechanisms to monitor any problems that might arise. In places where programs work, faculty avidly recruit students to science. They involve themselves and their departments in university-wide enterprises (a writing program at Fort Lewis); with community college instructors (at Cal State LA); by visiting local high schools (at UW-Eau Claire); or by mounting summer programs for high school students (at both Cal State LA and Trinity). In these faculty members' labs and classrooms the bottom line is *welcome*, with a promise of success. And the next bottom line is making sure that students in growing numbers *succeed* at learning science.

Fort Lewis College

Nestled among the high mountains of southwestern Colorado is a state-supported university that continues to call itself a college. Originally an Indian high school established in the 1880s, Fort Lewis College went through a series of transformations, from a junior college to a branch of Colorado State University. It was refounded in 1962, during the period of expansion of higher education, as an independent four-year state college with a liberal arts mission and a commitment to innovation.

Partly because of its mission, the Department of Chemistry attracted faculty members who had experience in four-year liberal arts institutions. Chairman Jim Mills was a student at Earlham in Indiana; Doreen Mehs, Colorado's 1991 CASE professor of the year, graduated from Harpur College; and John Ritchey's first teaching assignment was at Furman University in South Carolina. Ted Bartlett and Rod Hamilton, the department's organic chemists, also are liberal arts college graduates, as is Ron Estler who left a tenure-track position at a major research university to teach at Fort Lewis. Bartlett's early teaching experiences were at two strong liberal arts colleges in Minnesota. The newest member of the department, Les Sommerville, is a 1980 Fort Lewis alumnus, proof that the faculty believes in their program and its graduates. Many of the faculty could be called "refuseniks," intentionally rejecting the large, research-oriented university where, as Mehs puts it, "You can't do much harm or much good for most students." Mehs believes that it is the faculty's common small-college experience that contributes to the department's "unity of purpose and method."

The chemistry department, founded in the late 1960s, had its recruitment work cut out for it. In the 1970s, as Doreen Mehs remembers, "between zero and one student arrived at Fort Lewis intending to major in chemistry." Of the current sixteen majors per year average, one-third are from neighboring rural areas and two are American Indians.[1] The department has a good reputation among students. It's "where the action is," one told me. The "action" includes Friday seminars which students as well as faculty attend, and paid (summer) and unpaid research projects in which students can work with faculty. The department also boasts a congenial social atmosphere and an esprit de corps which students share.

That the chemistry program works is evidenced by: (1) its rate of recruitment and retention of majors–50 percent of the number of majors at Colorado State University with but 20 percent of Fort Collins' enrollment; 20 percent of the number of majors at the University of Colorado with fewer than 10 percent of Boulder's enrollment; (2) the number of Fort Lewis chemistry graduates who get jobs immediately upon graduation (23 percent) and who go on to graduate and professional schools (64 percent); (3) the college's standing among other institutions. In a survey of chemistry majors per thousand enrollees at public undergraduate

---

[1] The college-wide average is 10 percent.

institutions around the country, Fort Lewis ranked fifth.[2]

"There is nothing special about the curriculum," Jim Mills tells me in his typical understated fashion. Indeed, given the small size of the faculty, it is necessary to offer a fairly standard curriculum, though there is usually room for one new course for advanced students. Ideas tend to evolve in response to student needs and interests, such as a new offering in "consumer chemistry" for nonscience students built around the chemistry of everyday things. Designed by Ron Estler and taught by several members of the department, this course attracts students by the roomful to see clever demonstrations and upbeat "student-friendly" presentations. Following a brief introduction on how scientists think and on the risk assessment process in industry, students are taught the science needed to understand one kind of consumer product or concern, e.g., polymers and their ability to biodegrade. More science is added as discussion turns to more complex consumer products.

The course is not restricted to the nonmajors the department is determined to serve. Science majors looking for some applied chemistry take the course too, and discover new applications of the chemistry they have learned. Further, making chemistry part of the campus culture, says Estler, demonstrates to science and nonscience majors alike shared concerns.

Another new course does attract one or two majors a year. This is the freshman-sophomore writing course taught as a part of the college's "writing across the curriculum" program. Chemistry professor emeritus Merle Harrison was one of the architects of the program in the late 1960s, before these programs were nationally popular. Rod Hamilton's "science and society" is a perennial attraction for future majors. Doreen Mehs, who teaches "problems and puzzles" and "global change," believes that it is the strong student-faculty interaction that draws these writing students toward the chemistry major.

There is one undertaking which may be unique: Ted Bartlett's summer school course entitled "natural products from plants." Taught during Fort Lewis' "Innovative Month Program" in May, the course regularly attracts ten to fifteen chemistry and biology students who take it as an elective. It features independent study laboratory projects in the isolation, synthesis, and identification of biologically-active compounds from plant materials, particularly native plants of the Southwest. A high point of the course is a field trip, a backpack venture into a canyon area of

[2] In addition, the department was one of four winners of the Programs of Excellence Award given in 1991 by the Colorado Commission of Higher Education to encourage excellence in Colorado's postsecondary schools. If funding is approved during the 1992 legislative session, the department will receive $80,000.

Colorado near the Utah border where students gather specimens for laboratory study. The course attracts sophomores into the chemistry minor, and sometimes into the major.

Mills believes that the department's success in recruiting and retaining large numbers of students (more and more of them from out of state) comes from having a hand on the students' collective pulse. Teaching issues–what to teach, who to teach, and how to teach–are regularly discussed at department meetings. Chemistry majors are identified early and followed closely through their undergraduate (and even postgraduate) careers.

Because there are no graduate students at Fort Lewis, undergraduates use new instruments early, often in the sophomore organic laboratory course. Said one transfer student speaking of the university she left, "You gave your sample to the TA who put it through the NMR. Here we get on the NMR ourselves." The absence of a graduate program also means (as at UW-Eau Claire) that there are places for undergraduates in faculty members' laboratories. During summers, this translates into $2,500 student stipends paid for partly out of faculty grants and augmented by college funds. The recent award of a Howard Hughes biomedical development grant of $800,000 will help support more students and faculty in biomedical research.[3]

Success also comes from pragmatism and flexibility. "Teaching must fit teacher as well as student," department chairman Mills believes. It is important that a professor wants to be teaching a particular course or sequence. Teaching assignments are almost entirely voluntary, but every faculty member teaches in the introductory course, although not every year. All faculty are considered good teachers and some flashy, and all get student reviews that exceed the campus norm. More importantly, students come out of the course with a favorable attitude, Mills adds.

Even though all students take the same introductory course, class sizes have been limited. The department quit using its 250-seat auditorium ten years ago, choosing to increase its work load by subdividing introductory chemistry into smaller sections. These are limited to seventy-five to eighty students, with some as small as twenty-five to thirty, and the average sixty. Efforts are made to coordinate sections so that there is a sense of community and so students get to know all the instructors. The department sees eighty as the *maximum* class size that permits adequate interaction between students and faculty, students and students.

The department stresses knowing the students. Personal attention is a Fort Lewis tradition and a selling point in recruiting. In chemistry this

---

[3] Fort Lewis College was one of ninety-nine schools invited to apply for Howard Hughes grants; forty-four received funding.

personal attention takes the form of help sessions for introductory classes, either weekly or at exam time, and often in the evening when the students–one-third of whom live on campus–have free time. Personal support is provided by these sessions, support that extends into the classrooms, and faculty get to know names and something personal about each student by the third or fourth week of the semester.

The students interviewed during a brief two-day visit to Fort Lewis recognize that all this attention contributes to what they call the "capturing business" in which Fort Lewis' chemistry department is openly engaged. In the case of potential majors it begins even before they arrive–in some cases even before they apply to the college. Early in the admissions cycle the chemistry department asks admissions for a computer search of possible applicants showing high math and science ACT or SAT scores. It doesn't matter at this stage what their declared interest may be, or even how serious they are about Fort Lewis. Faculty member John Ritchey writes each of them the first of a series of two letters, with information about chemistry at Fort Lewis. He encourages them to visit the campus and advises–as a high school guidance counselor might– what to look for in a college search. Ten days later prospects receive a second letter bringing them up-to-date on department activities, on where recent graduates have landed professionally, and on the department's new instrumentation and latest awards for teaching and research, and inviting them to visit the department upon arriving.

"We send out hundreds of letters each year," reports Ritchey. "Students remember them and their parents read them. When they finally do arrive on campus, they come to see us." "Is chemistry's aggressiveness perceived as unfair advertising?" I ask. Not at all, I am assured. Chemistry also produces and distributes a detailed handbook with information on the major, career opportunities in industry, and how to apply to graduate schools.

"Operation capture" continues unabashedly through chem 150, the introductory course for geology, pre-engineering, biology, and chemistry majors. Chem 150 is looked upon by the department as a recruiting opportunity. Sections are relatively small and teaching is personal. And, as the students recollect it, class usually begins with something "irrelevant to the lesson" but very relevant to recruitment like "how much money patent lawyers make," or "the birthday of some chemist," or an interesting display of some kind. Without this, John Ritchey believes, there would be few chemistry majors at Fort Lewis. "With all our efforts," he says, "we still start out with just one or two freshmen ready to major in chemistry. But because 250 students must take introductory chemistry and because we present our subject in an interesting manner, we end up with ten or fifteen majors. Best of all, once they are juniors, we lose none!"

Critics might say that chemistry is out to increase its market share of the students who might major in the other sciences. But is it attracting students who might not? While some Fort Lewis chemistry students are unmistakably committed "first tier" chemists and have had good high school preparation, others would, the department believes, be discouraged by their grades or discover a poor "fit" between themselves and science if they were studying elsewhere. The department directs much of its energy to such students. It sees small class size and personal help sessions as providing a combination of "consolation and encouragement." Faculty are always on the lookout for "any and all signs of talent, particularly in those who think they have none." This requires, says Chairman Mills, a positive, upbeat attitude, treating each class almost as if it were the "best class ever." Privately the department worries about student preparation and other problems, but there is no public moaning about how poor the students are.

This means that every student is encouraged to *think about* chemistry as a career. "We believe it's a faculty responsibility to discuss with each student what we think he or she can develop into, both as a Fort Lewis student and in their career after graduation," says Mills. While stressing that a major is a student's choice and that postcollege decisions should correspond to personal motivations, the chemistry faculty encourages most juniors and seniors to consider continuing their studies into graduate school. While a few students read this counseling as pressure, the faculty sees it as "making certain that students are aware of what they can make happen." What "they can make happen" is, in fact, not limited to graduate school, and the faculty makes sure they support majors seeking other opportunities, in teaching, for example, or in industry.

I find the results of this encouragement evident in my student interviews. John Rau tells me he hated chemistry in high school where he regularly got 40 percent on tests, but loved chem 150 (which he took as part of a pre-engineering requirement) because, he remembers, "it was pure chemistry, not applied." Rau is a student who doesn't learn much by himself from a book. He responds, rather, to lively lectures–particularly those which "get you to think"–illustrations, demonstrations, and the challenge of "digging for answers." It has taken him longer than his professors at Fort Lewis to recognize that he has a different learning style. For years he was mystified by the fact that although he wasn't very "scholastic," he "really liked science." Majoring in inorganic chemistry and destined for graduate study, Rau is confident that he has found the right field and will do well.

Career opportunities in chemistry are described in the introductory classes, which include anecdotal accounts of alumni activities, what this week's departmental visitor is doing, and other topics. Another exposure to postgraduate life is provided by the Friday afternoon chemistry talk by a visitor or by a senior student. Many visitors come to promote graduate study at their own universities. Some are from industry, and two or three each year are from government labs–Los Alamos National Laboratory, the nearest major scientific institution, is four hours away. Each of the year's dozen or so visitors spends an entire Friday in chemistry and lunches with a group of juniors and seniors. They provide information about where the discipline and the profession are heading and an informal appraisal of the department itself.

During the winter semester the Friday afternoon seminar may feature an hour-long talk, based on library research, by a senior. Since all seniors are required to prepare such a colloquium, the question-and-answer period following serves as a public test of their understanding of the material and its underlying fundamental principles. There are always refreshments–whether a student or a visitor is the featured speaker–and afterwards some students and faculty drift downtown for more social-izing. The Friday afternoon "happening" builds momentum during the school year. Freshmen and sophomores discover that, "while the rest of the campus starts weekend partying, something interesting and enter-taining is going on in chemistry."

The seminar I attend is offered by Janet Grissom, a natural products synthesis chemist from the University of Utah. That Professor Grissom is a female is considered a plus. With 40 percent of its majors female, the department actively seeks women speakers. The fact that her university is paying her expenses is testimony that Fort Lewis graduates are attractive prospects for graduate study. Indeed, Fort Lewis students are applying for graduate work all over the country, though primarily in the West and Midwest. Whole contingents have gone to Indiana University, the University of Utah, and Montana State University. But more often they go to the best university for their interests and talents, without regard for their friends' destinations.

Janet Grissom's talk begins with a description of what a natural products chemist does, and why one would want to do this work. She proceeds to discuss the molecule taxol, which, she tells her audience, is in phase two clinical trials at the National Cancer Institute. Taxol offers real benefits in treating cancer, but is available only from the bark of the Pacific yew tree. With 12,000 trees needed to produce enough for clinical trials, it is imperative the compound be synthesized in the laboratory. So one reason a natural synthetic chemist wants to work on natural com-pounds is their utility. Another is the "pure pleasure" of working with novel structures; a third is to develop interesting new synthetic methods; and a fourth, always in the mind of a research chemist, Grissom empha-sizes, is to discover interesting and unanticipated chemistry.

Her seminar continues with a discussion of the work in which she is currently involved, and ends with photographs of her group, of the chemistry building at Utah, and of some of the snow-covered canyons that give Salt Lake City its scenic character. Throughout Grissom is at pains to demonstrate that chemistry is a human endeavor, that there are real people–not much different from the audience–working on the problem. When there are not too many questions from students at the end, the professors take the lead, as several have expertise in synthesis and natural products chemistry, and a lively discussion ensues. Later Grissom has dinner with the faculty and, the next morning (a Saturday), breakfast with some organic chemistry students.

The Friday afternoon seminar is budgeted at $1,000 per year out of department, ACS student affiliate chapter, and vice presidential funds. Sometimes the speaker's home institution pays the freight; other times, I am told, the department faculty reach into their own pockets to help defray expenses.

While students in the introductory course are not (yet) among frequent attendees, they cannot help but hear about these Friday sessions from upperclass lab assistants and in the chemistry study room. That study room, incidentally, with its coffeepot, refrigerator, and microwave oven, is the center of the department. Visiting, tutoring, studying, counseling, and lunching all go on there. Faculty wander in and out. The chalkboard serves as a message center, a key factor in helping students feel part of a community. Open from early morning until 10 P.M. or midnight, it is a place where students working on a problem often shout out a question for anyone in the vicinity to answer.

Summer research at Fort Lewis is on the upswing as federal and other agencies have offered more funding for research at undergraduate institutions. During the 1980s Ted Bartlett and one or two other faculty would be occupied with funded research during any summer. In recent years the number has increased to five or six, a level of activity that increases the pressure for modern equipment. The department has been aggressively writing proposals and soliciting donations to obtain the equipment, and the college has been generous in providing matching money. As a result, Fort Lewis may be one of the better equipped undergraduate departments in the region.[4] Their efforts continue with a new biochemistry lab development program headed by new faculty member Les Sommerville.

In the center of the chemistry department is a laser lab that would be the envy of most undergraduate institutions. Built in stages by Estler,

---

[4] Recent acquisitions supported by the NSF ILI program include a GC-MS, a high field FT NMR, and an FT/IR.

Mills, and Mehs, the spectroscopists in the department, the lab features three lasers and accompanying computers, lenses, and oscilloscopes, along with a time-of-flight mass spectrometer. The latter was paid for by an NSF grant and built by Estler's research students. Acquiring equipment and keeping it maintained has consumed a significant portion of departmental attention over the years. The resident full-time lab coordinator is Carl Stransky, a professional chemist, who makes sure that the equipment provides something more than ambience, and is used to maximum benefit by students and faculty alike.

The range of expectations for new faculty is considerable, something newcomer Sommerville discovered when being interviewed for his position. The most important qualification is "excellence in teaching," or, as it is written in the department's tenure document, the clear prospect of excellent teaching.[5]

> Most people can be good teachers on their best days. We want
> . . . people who are good even on a bad day or during a bad
> year. We seek some level of undeniable excellence, whether
> it be in classroom style, indefatigable nurturing, or pedagogi-
> cal insight. There also must be an irrepressible love for nature
> and science, to instill in our students a lifelong science
> interest.

In addition, the department expects new members to "have the professional drive to stay alive and functioning on the undergraduate scene." This means being able to find funding for research, including summer research with students, preferably at Fort Lewis. The department, however, also recognizes the contribution to its program from research ties to Los Alamos National Laboratories. Leadership in this area has come from Ritchey and Estler, who have worked summers at LANL for many years and provide opportunities for Fort Lewis students to assist in research there.

Another qualification any new hire must have, as described in the department's tenure document, is the "interpersonal skills required to furnish leadership in some component of the department's operations and to represent the department to the rest of the college and our professional community." An invaluable strength of the Department of Chemistry at Fort Lewis is the unity of goals and commitment it enjoys as a faculty. For this reason, the department is unwilling to risk its esprit de corps even for a "star." "No faculty member," says the tenure document, "can be so good that they add to the department while detracting from our ability to work together." Strong words!

---

[5] From "Observations Regarding Tenure for Chemistry Faculty," prepared by the department.

The payoff is high departmental morale. In the words of the department chairman:

> I cannot capture on paper the energy and enthusiasm in our department. Our department operates more by consensus and cooperation than by political posturing and competing. We have a collective sense of humor, grounded in a unity of purpose and a respect, even fondness, for one another. Being upbeat and enthusiastic about science as an intellectually satisfying enterprise and about a chemistry career as an enjoyable, worthwhile life-style is essential to our department's sense of well-being.

To underscore the importance of "attitude" toward students and science, one observes that on the department's student opinion questionnaires used in every course, there is always a question about "instructor enthusiasm." Common responses are "can't believe the enthusiasm . . . really loves this stuff . . . helped me get interested in the course."

Excerpts from student questionnaires reveal that the faculty are supportive: "I am a [returnee to school] and was worried about doing well. [The instructor] made all of us feel worthy." "Understanding that most of us are not science majors and couldn't or wouldn't dream of being such, he still treated us as intelligent adults." "We are free to ask any question and he calls on us immediately . . . always stimulates my mind." "After class I was always thinking [about] what if [questions] and I could always ask about my ideas." "Extremely knowledgeable about analytical chemistry. . . . A student can ask her a question any time and get a clear answer." "A genius on the subject, yet takes plenty of time to explain his thinking so we can follow what he is doing." And so on.

Conclusion

The question for science education is whether a program like this is exportable. Instead of discussing this, however, the faculty wants to tell me how "unique" Fort Lewis is. I explain that for my purposes what is typical about Fort Lewis College may be more interesting than what is unique. From Doreen Mehs I get the following analysis: Unlike the selective private institutions from which so many of the faculty came, Fort Lewis College is underfunded, nonselective in its student body, lower in status, lacking in endowment. What makes up for this, insists Mehs, is commitment and vision. "All we have," she says, "is a faculty." Since most of the students at Fort Lewis are anything but teacher-proof, it is critical that they have a "satisfying learning experience." That students at the larger universities need this, too, is addressed by the comments of Pam Fischer, a Fort Lewis alumna now in the Ph.D. program in chemistry at the University of Oregon.

> I entered Fort Lewis as an English/journalism major intend-
> ing to stay for one or two years and then to transfer to the
> University of Colorado at Boulder. While taking chem 150 as
> a distribution requirement, after not enjoying chemistry in
> high school, I found myself in Ron Estler's section and it was
> he who turned the light bulb on. . . . The classes were
> challenging and the material difficult and highly technical,
> but the interaction between the professor and the students
> made it fun. . . .

Jim Mills believes that it is attention to the day-to-day detail of running a department for undergraduates that makes the difference. Like myself, Mills discounts the "experimental model" and educational innovation per se. He is at pains to explain to me what the department is *not*:

> We chemistry faculty don't see ourselves as innovators so
> much as "program builders." The faculty has a five-year plan
> filled mostly with continuing improvements, to be steadily
> pursued as time and opportunity allow. Our innovations
> tend to be small. We are neither trendy nor high tech with
> video disks, software packages, computer-assisted instruc-
> tion, etcetera. Although Estler and Bartlett have contributed
> papers to chemical education sessions at national ACS meet-
> ings, we primarily attend sessions in our subdisciplines. . . .

What drives the department, in his words, is a different set of goals.

> We are a strategic department. We try hard to judge which
> changes will work and which will not, given local conditions.
> This means we must know who our students are and we must
> know who we really are so that proposed changes will work
> with the students and faculty alike. Grand designs tend to be
> left behind on the departmental table. . . .

The department's success is due in part to the fact that the faculty work well as a team, that they respect one another and enjoy friendly compe-tition. All of the faculty have enthusiasm for teaching and for their fields of expertise. They share responsibilities, some hustling for instrumenta-tion grants, others spending extra time developing courses. Some are active contributors to area primary and secondary school science pro-grams, while others are more heavily involved with Fort Lewis students in laboratory research, particularly in the summer. Mills continues:

> Our progress is not so much in innovation as in improve-
> ment. The curriculum is up-to-date, the lab equipment is

modern, and our students are aware of the latest develop-
ments in chemistry, but we are not inclined as a department
to embark on major experimental teaching projects. There is
a general faculty opinion that we do a better job with our
students each year.

And they do. In this institution, teamwork and passion produce cumulative improvement. Good teaching is viewed as an end in itself.

Trinity University

Trinity University is a midsized private liberal arts institution located
in San Antonio, Texas. Formed from three failing colleges following the
Civil War, Trinity was originally located in Waxahachie, Texas before
accepting an invitation to relocate to San Antonio in 1943. Known as a
quality regional institution, Trinity did not become a nationally recognized center of academic excellence until the 1980s. Richly endowed, the
university was one of the first to provide merit-based scholarships (1982)
that now bring sixty National Merit finalists each year to campus. In
recent *U.S. News and World Report* studies Trinity is ranked first among
comprehensive universities in the Southwest.

Science was not Trinity's principal strength prior to the 1980s, and
science majors entered medical school or industry rather than graduate
school. The '80s brought changes that created excitement in science at a
time when, nationally, student interest was declining. In 1989 Trinity
graduates from all departments received seven National Science Foundation graduate fellowships, placing fourteenth among U.S. colleges and
universities in awards per capita. The Department of Chemistry exem-
plifies the dramatic changes that have occurred. Between 1970 and 1985
an average of seven majors graduated per year and fewer than two per
year entered graduate school in the chemical sciences. Most pursued
medicine and some went directly into chemical industry. By the end of
the 1980s, in contrast, the number of chemistry majors had nearly tripled.
An average of seven students per year were entering graduate school in
chemistry or biochemistry, and in one two-year period five Trinity
University chemistry majors received prestigious NSF graduate fellowships, nearly 5 percent of the total awarded nationally.

When I reviewed the factors that contributed to this change, I was
reminded of economist Walt Rostow's characterization of economic
development, a rapid "takeoff" following a period during which an
infrastructure builds. Ronald Calgaard, the current president, came to
the university in 1979 with a determination to recruit the best faculty and
better students. In five years, from 1981 to 1986, the average combined

SAT scores of Trinity students increased from just under 1,100 to over 1,200. During that same period, a seventh member was added to the chemistry department in the person of Mike Doyle, who came to Trinity from Hope College in Michigan where there is a long tradition of excellence in chemistry education. Hope is the place where the "Council on Undergraduate Research Newsletter" was first published, of which Doyle is the editor. In the early 1980s, Doyle remembers, chemistry at Trinity was ". . . a reaction waiting to happen."

A catalyst was added and the reaction occurred. President Calgaard was extremely supportive, providing $1.5 million to replace inadequate facilities. The Semmes Foundation created Doyle's chair, and instrument acquisition over three years was made possible by grants totaling $700,000 from NSF, the Keck Foundation, the Camille and Henry Dreyfus Foundation, Hewlett-Packard, IBM, Research Corporation, and an additional $300,000 from Trinity itself. Then there was a significant increase in research support to chemistry faculty from outside sources.

Such changes and acquisitions are more common in larger, research-oriented universities. The visitor to Trinity University is struck by how much *undergraduate* chemistry students benefit from sophisticated instrumentation. In the summer of 1990 when I made a site visit to Trinity, forty-one students were performing research with chemistry faculty. Ten had just completed their freshman year and many were on their way toward being converted to the discipline. About the same number were similarly engaged a year later.

Undergraduate Research

We need only to listen to the students to hear how undergraduate research contributes toward recruitment and retention. A 1991 graduate, Danny arrived at Trinity with interests somewhere "between biology and chemistry." In the summer of his freshman year he joined Nancy Mills' research group and has been doing research with her ever since. It was this research experience, Danny recalls, that caused him to choose chemistry as a major and as a career.[6] For Scott, raised by a physician father in a town with a university that emphasizes premedicine, the decision was not so easy. As he tells it,

> I entered Trinity with a rather limited view of the nature of science. My initial curriculum emphasized premed and I didn't begin actively participating in research until the summer following my sophomore year. Although I entered the

---

[6] From student testimonials collected by the Department of Chemistry.

research lab with the attitude of a summer employee, by the
end of that summer I knew that research was what I wanted
to pursue as a career.

Scott's research collaboration began with Benjamin Plummer on
photochemistry, light-induced reactions of organic compounds. Later he
did genetics research with a biology professor (William Stone), returning
to a chemistry laboratory in his junior year and, on several occasions
before graduation, presenting research papers at scientific meetings. A
paper, coauthored with Plummer, appeared in *Tetrahedron Letters*. Scott
won an NSF Graduate Fellowship on graduation and went on to pursue
a Ph.D. degree at Caltech.

Another convert from premedicine is Jack, whose research experience
began the summer before his junior year. After taking a year of organic
chemistry with Mike Doyle, Jack was persuaded that ". . . chemistry, not
medicine, would be my lifelong discipline." His first research project,
assigned by Doyle, centered on free carbenes. Even though free carbenes
have a history of virtually nonexistent synthetic utility, by the end of the
summer Jack was able to prepare free carbene-derived products in a 90
percent yield. Thereafter, he was able to establish the relative reactivities
of various substrates, using high field NMR spectroscopy in tandem with
gas chromatography. Collaboration with Matthew Platz of Ohio State
University resulted in a paper in *Tetrahedron Letters*, one of five he
eventually published based on research with Doyle at Trinity. What Jack
remembers most about collaborative research are both the "personal
dimension of discovery" and the "rewards of teamwork." For Tom,
another recent graduate who holds an NSF graduate fellowship at
Harvard University, undergraduate research laid the groundwork for
the discoveries in biological chemistry he is making in graduate school.

Revising the Standard Curriculum

Research is not the only special experience available to Trinity students. In 1988 the Department of Chemistry taught the classical general
chemistry course for the last time. This course, virtually identical to those
found at the vast majority of colleges and universities, is basically a
survey. Doyle calls it a "travelogue through the myriad topics that
educators, exam manufacturers, and textbook authors have determined
to be essential to every student's college experience. If this is week four,
the topic is stoichiometry; week five covers the essentials of thermodynamics." For Trinity students, the faculty came to believe the standard
course was a review of what most of them had already learned in high
school. For too many (Mike Doyle again), "general chemistry was simply

asking for four significant figures instead of the three demanded in high school."

However unsatisfactory it was, replacing the foundation course was not to be done lightly.[7] Indeed, the revolution was preceded by several attempts at reforming the introductory course. For three years, beginning in 1985, the chemistry faculty experimented with alternative approaches, each a variant on the general chemistry theme. But none of them produced the desired result, namely "generating enthusiasm for chemistry among students." When these attempts failed, William Kurtin, then department chair, pushed the faculty to consider a "more drastic change." That drastic change involved replacing the standard general chemistry courses with basic courses in analytical and organic chemistry.

The fact that the Trinity faculty included three organic chemists (Doyle, Mills, and Plummer) willing to undertake the instruction of students at the introductory level made it possible to construct a new course (without outside funding or faculty release time) with some confidence that such a change would be acceptable to the ACS.

Instead of a full-year course in general chemistry, Trinity University now offers a one-semester course in analytical chemistry emphasizing quantitative analysis, followed by the first of a two-semester sequence in organic (and bioorganic) chemistry. The first course emphasizes the quantitative aspects of chemistry that are also of particular interest to students in engineering and physics; the second is qualitative in nature and is especially attractive to those headed toward the biological sciences. The change, says Doyle, is meaningful: students whose motivation and capabilities allow them to excel in qualitative, conceptual areas love the change from analytical chemistry. Those whose quantitative skills allow them to excel in the first course are also attracted to the unified logic of the second course.

Enrollments following the introduction of the new courses testify to their appeal. With the old curriculum a first-year class of 160 sent fifty-five students to the second-year course in bioorganic chemistry and only forty-five of the initial 160 completed the two-year sequence. Now, of the 160 who begin with the introduction to quantitative analysis, eighty remain at the start of the second year and seventy stay through the end of the two-year sequence.

"In this curricular approach," says Doyle, echoing Philip Morrison of MIT, "less is more." Rather than beginning with the entire periodic table as in general chemistry, the new curriculum focuses on only a few elements, and subsequent courses build upon this foundation. Student

---

[7] See Seyhan Ege's account of reorganization of the University of Michigan's undergraduate chemistry sequence during the same period (chap. 4).

performance on standardized tests has not suffered from this approach.

Another revision was to expand laboratories for students from three to six hours per week beginning the second year, and to integrate the subdisciplines–organic chemistry with inorganic chemistry and analytical chemistry with physical chemistry. The key to the success of this "laboratory-rich program" (Doyle's term) is student access to modern instrumentation usually found only in professional laboratories devoted to chemical, biomedical, or environmental analyses. Although acquisition costs are high, over $1 million at Trinity, the benefits in student understanding of modern chemical science, the faculty believes, are "enormous."

Today at Trinity one rarely sees a test tube in a chemistry laboratory. Analyses are performed on milligram or smaller amounts and not on the gram scale required three decades ago. Students are encouraged to undertake independent laboratory study as early as their first year, and can join faculty research groups through a one-credit course in research techniques and applications. The course requires students to learn the chemical and instrumental analysis techniques required by a particular research problem. These same research questions may continue to engage students during the summer or the next year as they move into "independent research in chemistry and biochemistry," a course that encourages even more autonomy.[8] These experiences directly aid students in their other coursework. Says one:

> The biggest benefit I received was the lab experience. I did not have as many problems with the experiments as my peers in my first semester organic class because I had worked with most of the glassware, and had handled some of the reagents. I finished the experiments in less time and was more efficient. I have always enjoyed lab work, and when I saw that I was pretty good at it, my motivation was sparked.

The Trinity University chemistry program is not perfect. There are deficiencies, some due to limitations in faculty size (seven) and laboratory space. The number of advanced courses has been restricted to five, which frustrates some students who desire more. There is only one track in the chemistry curriculum and all students take the same introductory sequence whether they intend to major in biology, engineering science,

[8] For a review of undergraduate research in chemistry education, see James N. Spencer and Claude H. Yoder, "A Survey of Undergraduate Research over the Past Decade," *Journal of Chemical Education*, Vol. 58, October 1981, p. 780; Jerry R. Mohrig and Gene G. Wubbels, "Undergraduate Research as Chemical Education," *Journal of Chemical Education*, Vol. 61, June 1984, p. 507; and "The Chemical Education of Butchers and Bakers and Public Policy Makers," *Journal of Chemical Education*, Vol. 61, June 1984, p. 509.

or any other discipline requiring chemistry. Students who want to do research during the academic year often find themselves in crowded laboratories vying for available space; however, this was to be alleviated by the summer of 1992 through a renovation made possible by an NSF grant.

Since few freshmen who undertake research are productive their first year, their summer stipends and research supplies are a gamble for their faculty mentors. External research grants, which provide most of the funding for faculty-student research, are based in large part on productivity. When a student does not continue with a project or contribute to its development, its future is jeopardized. Still, without early beginnings, many students now majoring in chemistry and intending to pursue the chemical sciences as a career would have been lost. The dropout rate for students who begin chemistry research in their freshman year is about 30 percent, but this doesn't mean they are lost to science. Many of them decide to pursue other science majors as a result of their exposure to research.

Conclusion

Research is as strong a catalyst for students' development at Trinity as it is at Fort Lewis and UW-Eau Claire. But perhaps even more important is the attention they receive from faculty in the research lab, in their courses, and in the extracurricular activities that the departments provide. The payoff is in the numbers. Where fewer than one out of 100 introductory chemistry students at large state universities typically selects chemistry as a major, the rate is at least six times that at departments like Trinity's. The lesson from this institution is that an infusion of money and personnel at the right time, in a setting already predisposed to change, makes a difference.

4
Structure and Reactivity
Introductory Chemistry at the University of Michigan

It is tempting to argue that what is possible at four-year state universities and independent colleges may not be so at larger research institutions. After all, the smaller colleges have no graduate clientele to serve or employ as teaching assistants. Critics will assert that pedagogical innovation is easy where class size can be controlled and the first two years of science are unencumbered by large projects, faculty travel, consulting, and the constant need to write grants to support the infrastructure. So when a major research university manages to revitalize its undergraduate program in science–even though the overhaul is principally curricular–that change should be examined.

The Scope of the Overhaul

The process began at the University of Michigan in the 1980s with a four-year period of self-examination followed by the creation, testing, and installation of a new introductory course in organic chemistry, followed in turn by a complete revision of upper division chemistry courses. Professor Seyhan Ege, associate chair of the Department of Chemistry, worked with her curriculum committee and a group of like-minded colleagues to spearhead the change. Her story is loaded with lessons about the process of change for those who would reform undergraduate science elsewhere.[1]

---

[1] The material in this chapter borrows heavily from a talk by Seyhan N. Ege and Brian P. Coppola, "The New Undergraduate Curriculum at the University of Michigan," given at the Alliance for Undergraduate Education meeting, Ann Arbor, Mich., April 7, 1990, and from an unpublished paper on the same topic entitled "The Liberal Arts of Chemistry: The New Curriculum at the University of Michigan." I have also benefited from reading and/ or hearing several additional presentations about the new curriculum: (1) Ege: Symposium on "Chemistry at Four-Year Colleges and Universities" at the 23rd Great Lakes

The decision to develop a new course sequence was motivated (as Ege and her associate Brian P. Coppola tell it) by familiar concerns–the feared shortfall of science and engineering professionals, student dissatisfaction with introductory chemistry, an increasing number of advanced placement students who were postponing their first course in college (organic) chemistry until their sophomore year, and a study by the local Women in Science program pointing to the first year course as the discouraging factor for women.[2]

At least as critical to their thinking was their accumulated experience teaching introductory organic chemistry to large (about 800) groups of second-year undergraduate students. The majority of these students had just completed their first year of college chemistry, a traditional general chemistry course. From anecdotal evidence, Ege and Coppola concluded that second-year students were bringing with them from high school and first-year chemistry many false notions about science in general and chemistry in particular. For one, they acted as though "science is certain and answers are knowable." Ege and Coppola were further struck, as have been many before them, that

> ... teaching students to solve problems about chemistry is not equivalent to teaching them about the nature of matter. Students can solve problems about gases without knowing anything about the nature of a gas, problems about limiting reagents without understanding the nature of chemical change.[3]

Introductory general chemistry, then, became their first focus for change. There were going to be at least four curricular problems to solve. High schools, Ege says, teach much of what is now taught in college level introductory chemistry, not in as much depth, not as well, but enough so

---

Regional Meeting of the American Chemical Society, May 31, 1990; (2) Ege: Symposium on Microscale Organic Chemistry Laboratory at the 11th Biennial Conference on Chemical Education, August 7, 1990; (3) Ege and M.D. Curtis: Symposium on Perspectives in Advanced Placement Chemistry at that same conference; and (4) PEW Midstates Consortium Curriculum Workshop, University of Chicago, April 12-14, 1991. More important and much appreciated are the conversations I was able to schedule with Seyhan Ege in Chicago, in Albion, Mich., and, including Brian Coppola, in Ann Arbor; and a written narrative of the history of the program provided by Ege in answer to my written questions.

[2] Jean D. Manis, Nancy G. Thomas, Barbara F. Sloat, and Cinda-Sue Davis, "An Analysis of Factors Affecting Choices of Majors in Science, Mathematics, and Engineering at the University of Michigan." CEW Research Report No. 23, Center for Continuing Education of Women (1989).

[3] Taken by Ege from Susan C. Nurrenbern and Miles Pickering, "Concept Learning Versus Problem Solving: Is There a Difference?" *Journal of Chemical Education,* 64 (1987), pp. 508-510.

that students feel they have "learned this all before."[4] Another problem is that general chemistry has become weighted toward the physical to the exclusion of descriptive chemistry–the qualitative understanding of chemical concepts. Further, general chemistry is fragmented by the large number of topics, Ege explains. "Students have no opportunity to build in-depth understanding of a few topics using increasingly sophisticated chemical models." Finally, evidence that women students were responding negatively to science courses made Ege feel that it was "urgent to try to design courses that more accurately reflect what chemists do."[5]

Designing Structure and Reactivity

Over the years the Michigan organic chemistry faculty had developed ways of teaching that emphasized general concepts and mechanistic similarities rather than content, reactions, and synthesis. Students responded positively, providing evidence of skills in analogical reasoning, pattern finding, and sorting out relevant facts in problem solving. These skills helped them in their other courses. The organic chemists used their small honors sections (in the second-year course) to test ideas about how students learn and how independent they could be in the laboratory. Ege recalls: "The more feedback we got, the more clearly we saw that it was necessary to make the development of skills–the skills of the liberal arts– an explicit part of our teaching." It became apparent to Ege and her colleagues that the same methods applied to a modified content would provide an ideal first-year course in chemistry.

When it came to content, they reasoned not only that less taught would be more learned, but that the reverse is also true: more would always be "less" when it came to student mastery.[6] Ege and Coppola write:[7]

> We each have lists of topics that should be required knowledge for those who study chemistry. But the content of chemistry has exploded. . . . There are scientists doing chemistry who call themselves molecular biologists or materials scientists. We cannot teach all of the content that is necessary

[4] Ege, quoting Betty Wruck and Jesse Reinstein, "Chemistry Instruction: Observations and Hypotheses," *Journal of Chemical Education*, 66 (1989), p. 1029.

[5] Nancy W. Brickhouse, Carolyn S. Carter, and Kathryn C. Scantlebury, "Women and Chemistry: Shifting the Equilibrium Toward Success," *Journal of Chemical Education*, 67 (1990), pp. 116-118.

[6] The idea that "less is more" in science teaching is attributed to MIT physicist Philip Morrison. See P. Morrison, "Less May be More," *American Journal of Physics*, 32 (1964), p. 441.

[7] Ege and Coppola, "The Liberal Art of Chemistry: The New Curriculum at the University of Michigan," unpublished paper, p.4.

> for those who will use chemistry professionally. It is impor-
> tant . . . to give our students the tools to recognize chemical
> problems when they see them, . . . to find data, to analyze
> data, and [teach them] how to use data in the solution of
> problems.

Ege and Coppola weren't referring exclusively to quantitative problems. In the homework assignments and on exams the new course would
have students explore "the actual molecular phenomena that the problems represented [instead of just looking for] a quantitative answer."
Further, the new course would be an immersion experience.[8]

> In choosing intensive immersion in one area, we moved away
> from the idea that the freshman year is . . . when foundations
> for all other areas of chemistry should be laid. We decided
> that a significant number of students would have . . . the
> fundamental concepts and language . . . that we could build
> on, reinforcing earlier concepts by moving into new areas
> that required their application, rather than by reviewing the
> concepts, albeit more rigorously, in old contexts.

In designing the new curriculum, she and her colleagues decided that
principles of *structure and reactivity* were the key to understanding
everything from materials to living organisms and should form the basis
for introductory chemistry. Also, they decided that "real problem solving" should be a component of the laboratory courses, even in year one.

The stage was set for the introduction of a new chemistry curriculum
with the following as its goals: to awaken the interest of students in the
chemical sciences and to retain more of them in the discipline; to integrate
early laboratory courses with lectures so as to emphasize method and
process; to encourage student participation in faculty research projects;
to develop new undergraduate programs in biochemistry, polymer
chemistry, and science education; and to make special efforts on behalf
of women and minority students.

Selling the Idea

Instead of allowing course content requirements to dominate the
planning process, Ege took the position that a highly diversified content
could provide the vehicle for introducing the "special ways" in which
chemists identify and solve problems involving transformations of
matter. It was one thing to convince her colleagues in chemistry that the
important concepts could be served by such a course, but it was just as

---

[8] Ibid.

necessary in a university like Michigan to persuade chemistry's outside clients as well. "I had to worry a great deal about content requirements," Ege said at an American Chemical Society symposium, "for we have a large engineering school. . . ."[9] The engineers wanted their students to take the same courses as chemistry majors. Indeed, the Michigan chemistry department has never had separate tracks either for engineers or for premeds, although there is one intermediate physical chemistry course meant mostly for materials scientists and geologists.

Investigating engineering requirements in chemistry before making changes, Ege was surprised when a colleague in chemical engineering told her there really weren't any. This perception proved correct. When she met with all the engineering program directors to explain the new chemistry courses and ask for input, she could not get anyone to tell her, "our students need to know this or they need to know that." For certification, engineers must take only one term of chemistry with lab. Requirements were no more specific than that.

Introductory chemistry, however, also serves premeds and biology majors. There might have been problems in persuading those departments to "buy in" to the change. But the biologists welcomed the more structured, qualitative approach Ege proposed for the first course. This, they decided, would better prepare students for the molecular component in introductory biology than traditional general chemistry. The biochemists and those involved in Michigan's accelerated Inteflex premed program (see page 64) also preferred the new sequence. They thought that a qualitative first course, followed by a third term with topics usually taught in first-year chemistry, would be good preparation for medical school biochemistry. Thus, while some in chemistry believed certain topics were indispensable because this is what departments outside of chemistry needed, the new curriculum worked well for most programs. "I think," says Ege reflecting on the process of getting other departments to agree, "we impose imaginary restrictions on ourselves."

Installing Structure and Reactivity

In the fall of 1989 the first 380 students (of 2,100 who start chemistry at the university each year) enrolled in structure and reactivity. By fall 1991 the number had climbed to 960, of whom 520 were first-year

[9] Ege's presentation and the panel response, dated August 26, 1990, is available from the Committee on Professional Training of the American Chemical Society. See also Coppola's presentation at the National Association for Research on Science Teaching, Lake Geneva, Wis., April 9, 1991, and at the American Chemical Society's twenty-first annual meeting, Atlanta, Ga., April 16, 1991.

students. Students are advised to take the new two-semester course if they score three or above on an advanced placement exam, or at the 70th percentile or above on a nationally administered high school chemistry examination administered during orientation to incoming students.[10] This means that those entering the course can be assumed to have had at least one year of high school chemistry within the past three years.[11]

The thrust of the course is not to convey facts but "the multiple and flexible ways," as Ege puts it, in which chemists explain chemical properties and predict the properties of unfamiliar species. The stress is on models and the processes by which chemists develop models to rationalize chemical phenomena. With organic chemistry the vehicle, the course aims at introducing students to how chemists think at the molecular level. Rapidly, it is hoped, students should be brought to the point where they can predict reaction results based on an understanding of the periodic properties of elements. "We strive to bring our students to a level where new observations may be viewed as redundant in the context of the conceptual model, rather than as another set of facts," Coppola adds.[12]

The Laboratory

The laboratory for structure and reactivity received as much attention from course designers as the content of the lectures. First tried out for several years as the honors section of sophomore organic chemistry, the laboratory was designed to avoid what Ege and Coppola call "the locked-step reproduction of preordained results." Like other reformers of general chemistry, they wanted to give students "authentic activity" without any sacrifice of technical instruction. Above all, they wanted to provide opportunities for self-correction—something often excluded from the introductory lab.

To accomplish this, students engage in open-ended activities in the structure and reactivity lab, making independent observations to solve individual (or group) problems. For example, in one exercise involving white solids, students are given twenty-seven vials containing nine

---

[10] "Cooperative Examination for High School Chemistry" designed jointly by the American Chemical Society and the National Science Teachers Association and administered by high school teachers as a final exam and by colleges as a placement exam.

[11] See Appendix A (p. 174) for a detailed chart of the prerequisites and course offerings in the new curriculum.

[12] Brian Coppola, "Learning in Undergraduate Chemistry Laboratory as an Apprenticeship," presented at the National Association for Research on Science Teaching, Lake Geneva, Wis., April 13, 1991, p. 2.

different substances (in triplicate sets). Each of the eighteen to twenty-four students in a laboratory section selects a vial. Their task is to figure out who else in class has the same substance they do. Then, provided with a set of authentic samples, they make identification by comparison. What constitutes a valid comparison becomes the key question in this lab, for in order to compare their data, the students have to develop their own systems and criteria. The lab stimulates cooperation, since students do their identification cooperatively. Together, rather than in competition, students develop their technical and observational abilities.[13]

After one term structure and reactivity students tackle problems with less and less guidance. A second-term assignment might be to read a recent journal article describing a new synthetic methodology and to test it on a variety of new substrates. Many of these laboratory exercises have been used at other institutions. Noteworthy at Michigan, however, is that the laboratory is integrated into the new course and nearly 1,600 students take it over two semesters.

Results

How well are students served by structure and reactivity? How much do they learn? How competent are they in comparison to peers in other first-year courses? The answer depends on what questions you ask and how you ask them, and what you expect students to know. In an early attempt to evaluate the laboratory, Brian Coppola set himself the task of comparing the oral responses of twenty-two structure and reactivity students (having had first-year chemistry), twenty traditional organic students (each with two years of college chemistry), and four "experts" (advanced graduate students and faculty members) to an open-ended identification question. A small capped vial containing about a milliliter of a clear colorless liquid (dichloromethane) was placed next to a tape recorder. The question to each participant: "What stepwise procedure would you use to determine the nature of the material in this vial?" Each time there was a response, the interviewer pressed forward with "what will you learn?" or "that didn't work, what next?"

Comparing the two groups of students and the experts, Coppola concluded that the students in the new first-year course held a more "expert conception" about the task than students in the traditional course.[14] The latter, he reported, focused mainly on identification, using

---

[13] In the laboratory, as in the course as a whole, students are graded on an absolute scale, not on a curve. Hence cooperation is in no way detrimental to their performance.

[14] Brian Coppola, "Learning in Undergraduate Chemistry . . . ," p. 13.

water solubility as structural evidence. Not one of the students in the traditional courses explicitly considered the homogeneity of the sample; all of the structure and reactivity enrollees did. The key, he thinks, was that structure and reactivity students have a more intimate association with a laboratory environment and a greater degree of confidence. They could also predict how much information one might get from a spectroscopic analysis; students who had taken the traditional courses were more tentative in their estimates.

To some extent, structure and reactivity students are primed for the kinds of questions Coppola asks in his evaluation. Ege and Coppola were determined from the outset that their examinations would not merely test the students' numerical competencies, but extend the teaching and learning tools of the course.[15] There are no multiple choice tests in structure and reactivity. Students are expected to produce their own answers. All examinations are graded by hand, partial credit is given, and comments are written. One question on a typical test requires the student to produce an answer in structural terms, while the very next one asks the student to draw a three-dimensional representation of a compound and show the expected bond angles. In the next, students are given data they are not expected to know–the example is not in the book and was not discussed in class–and asked to give a structural answer. Further down the page a structural explanation (in words) of a physical property is required.

Ege wants students to be able to produce both words and pictures. Exams are designed to ferret out students who have memorized a catch phrase, but who can't draw a picture to show they know what they are talking about. Exams feature compounds they have heard or read about (e.g., cocaine) and links to current research. Most important, while the data given in the tables attached to the exam are quantitative, students are asked to use those data to arrive at qualitative judgments.

The Classroom Climate

It is difficult to document changes in the classroom climate that accompanied curricular changes at Michigan because the course is so new. We do know Ege and her colleagues resolved to make the course encouraging and noncompetitive. They told students "we are here to help you succeed," and did not grade on a curve. They encouraged

---

[15] See Brian Coppola's report, "Studying the Structure and Reactivity Course: A Report from the End of the Second Year," available from Ege, and Appendix A (p. 175) of this volume for examples of examination questions used in the course.

students to study together. They also made senior faculty accessible to students in their first year by establishing student-faculty workshops one evening a week. Faculty were urged to model their own problem-solving strategies at these sessions.

As structure and reactivity becomes regularized through addition of faculty, more and more instructors will be able to apply the new pedagogical approach to their other courses. Already chem 130, the one-term general chemistry course for students who did not place into structure and reactivity or who want to start with a conventional class, is showing some changes. Although it resembles traditional general chemistry courses in its content and style, and features multiple choice examinations and grading on a curve, it now includes evening workshops for faculty and students.

From Course Innovation to Curriculum Reform

How did structure and reactivity come to be, and how was it possible to so radically alter the chemistry sequence? The political process that took place holds lessons for revitalizing science elsewhere.

In the early 1980s, Ege reports in her analysis, the organic chemistry faculty was already experimenting with the second-year course, so a critical mass of reform-minded faculty was in place. Then there was the existence (since 1972) of Inteflex, a seven-year integrated liberal arts and medical degree program. In the early years of Inteflex the chemistry department was asked to design special three-term general and organic courses. Much thinking went into what kind of chemistry was needed for these nonmajors. Ege's own experience in teaching them helped her decide to write an organic chemistry textbook that would emphasize the nature of reactivity in organic compounds, rather than rote learning of reactions.[16] The book is unusual in making acid-base chemistry the basis of further knowledge, which corresponds to the approach chosen for structure and reactivity.

As chair of the curriculum committee since 1981 and associate chair of the department after 1988, Ege was aware of both the strengths and weaknesses of Michigan's undergraduate program. Michigan offered students five tracks (including Inteflex), ranging from an honors class with fewer than 100 students with superior preparation, to another class of 100 which attracted those underprepared in math and science and adult returnees. In between were two large general chemistry sections of about 700 students each, one for those who did well on the ACS test, and

---

[16] Seyhan N. Ege, *Organic Chemistry*, 2nd ed. (Lexington, Mass.: D.C. Heath, 1989).

one for those who did not. The strength of the program was that all of the tracks were designed to bring all of the students to organic chemistry in the third term.[17]

Change was initiated not with a grand design, but with individual discussions with organic chemists about starting better prepared students with an introductory course based on organic chemistry. Ege was not naive about the dislocations that would follow such a change. In the immediate short run, she warned, the new plan would increase teaching loads for the organic chemists in the department, as many of them would be shifted from second-year to first-year courses. An absolute increase in student enrollment could also be expected, since geologists and engineers who did not normally enroll in organic chemistry would now be in the first-term course. The biology department and chemical engineering were also approached to find out if they could foresee problems with the plan. Still, when Ege circulated a preliminary proposal, she got little response. There the matter rested for a couple of years. Germination would take time.

During this period, a new chemistry building with laboratories for general and organic chemistry was authorized and a new chairman, M. David Curtis, was appointed. The question of equipment for the new building raised the issue of curriculum again. Equipping any curriculum would most likely set the pattern for some time, so if changes were to be made, this would be a good time to make them. Curtis agreed and decided to have "new courses to teach" in the new laboratories.

As associate chair Ege had primary responsibility for the undergraduate curriculum and for the department's teaching. That position, the pending construction of new labs (and the need to finance them), made change more palatable, and she again set about persuading the faculty of the merits of the new curriculum. With a plan put forward by the curriculum committee and strong support from the chair, the faculty agreed in 1988 to a comprehensive overhaul of the curriculum from freshman to senior year.

When the move to the new building was finally made in the summer of 1989, the $300,000 available from the university for laboratory start-up bought FT-infrared spectrophotometers, gas chromatographs, and an FT nuclear magnetic spectrometer, as well as additional balances and pH meters. The College of Literature, Science and the Arts loaned the department money to convert to microscale equipment, an investment

---

[17] The honors section used a higher level textbook and had an accompanying laboratory. Better prepared nonhonors students had a general chemistry laboratory with the standard types of inorganic and quantitative experiments. Less well-prepared students were given an extra lecture hour per week and waited until the second term of general chemistry to take lab.

that Ege says is already paying for itself in smaller quantities of chemicals and in disposal of waste. Since students need only small amounts of chemicals for their experiments, it is now possible to assign individualized laboratory problems.

The first 380 students entered structure and reactivity (chemistry 210/211) in 1989. Planning for the new chem 230 (which would pick up 210/211 students in their third semester) and the chem 130 course (for students who don't place into 210/211) brought in physical and inorganic chemists like Marian Hallada and Christer Nordman. Chem 230, now called "physical chemical principles and applications," includes much of the content of the traditional second-term general chemistry course but, since it enrolls students who have completed structure and reactivity, it can be taught at a higher level than general chemistry. Students not going on in science can take it as a terminal course.[18] Chemistry 230 also serves as an additional elective for engineering students. For chemistry majors, cellular molecular biologists, and chemical engineers, the new curriculum makes it possible, for the first time, to take a course in "real" inorganic chemistry (chem 302), designed by Vincent Pecoraro, as early as the second year.[19]

Even after the new first course was formally adopted, momentum was not permitted to falter. In the fall of 1989, the department held an all-day workshop to discuss the new curriculum and plan for additional changes. Ege's colleagues, busy designing second-year courses, kept her up to date on their progress, so that she could see how their ideas fit into the overall plan. By the end of 1992 winter term, the department had entirely moved to the new curriculum.

Ege continued to meet regularly with client schools and departments, biology, geology, and the schools of pharmacy and engineering, so that they would know what was happening in the first-year courses and what to expect of their students as they moved through the new curriculum. Ege would explain the nature and rationale of the new chemistry curriculum and help departments identify the courses that would best meet their students' needs.[20] While she was always willing to talk to program directors and curriculum committees, she did not accommo-

---

[18] Most science majors take chemistry 340, a more advanced integrated physical chemistry and analytical chemistry course, taught for the first time in 1991 by Mark Meyerhof, Don Gordus, and Tom Dunn.

[19] See Appendix A, p. 174, for a detailed chart of Michigan's new chemistry sequences.

[20] Except for chemical engineering, the engineers were more interested in the existence of a five-credit package of chemistry lectures and lab than in specific content. But scheduling requirements have to be dealt with: engineers often need to split lecture from lab; the new course with its associated lab does not always fit student schedules.

date chemistry's changes entirely to clients' needs, real or perceived. She felt strongly, as she puts it, that ". . . it was those 'needs' that have held us frozen, unable to make a move in changing curriculum." The department took the view that they, as chemists, were best qualified to judge where the discipline was going and the mental skills necessary to understand and work with new chemical knowledge. Given that the content of chemistry has exploded beyond what is teachable in four terms, let alone in a one-term service course, it was for chemistry, not its clients, to determine the specific content of its courses.

Besides the start-up costs for the new building and the loan for equipment changeovers, no financial support came to the department for the implementation of the new plan. Once the department embarked on curricular change, however, industrial and college support was forthcoming: $250,000 from Warner Lambert-Parke Davis, $100,000 from Amoco, $20,000 from BASF-Wyandotte, and a GC-MS (value about $56,000) from Hewlett-Packard. The college provided funds to upgrade standard equipment such as pH meters, and NSF gave $200,000 after the program was well on its way. The money is being used to buy more instruments for structure and reactivity courses as enrollments increase. It is also being used to equip three new upper-level laboratory courses.

Change in the introductory course is having its effect. As students in the new curriculum learn to design their own experiments and to think analytically, they become impatient with the content and the pedagogy of the courses that follow. Undergraduate participation in departmental research has grown from an average fifteen to twenty students per term to fifty to fifty-five, and many have joined research groups in all areas of chemistry as early as their first or second semester of college.

"Change isn't easy, and it's difficult to say whether it's been 'good' or 'bad'," Ege concedes. "What are the measures of success? What weight do we give to a lack of specific knowledge on the one hand, and to the eagerness with which students attach themselves to research groups on the other?" The answers will be years in coming, but the faculty intends to track the number of students who stay in the sciences, the number who go to graduate school, and the kinds of records they compile. Already the number of students who convert to a major in chemistry during their first year has grown from one to four per year to fourteen to eighteen.

The department is particularly sensitive to the need to do a better job of attracting and retaining women and minority students. One indication that the new curriculum is succeeding is the rate at which students from the small winter term section of chemistry 210/211 (which, for various reasons, has a large number of returning women students and minorities) apply for summer research programs immediately following their first course in chemistry–four in the first year.

Will the New Curriculum Survive?

Crucial to long-term success is whether the new curriculum provides a viable pathway to B.S. degrees in chemistry and then to higher degrees and/or jobs. Will students who complete a curriculum that emphasizes integrated laboratory courses and undergraduate research be as successful as earlier graduates in getting jobs and completing graduate school? How will faculty continue to respond, once the curriculum is no longer "new?" "There is nothing magical about the new curriculum," Ege insists. Its implementation was the result of a small number of people who put a lot of effort and energy into it. But she fears it could freeze into dogma as soon as energy and interest stop flowing. The research faculty must continue to contribute. They will, she thinks, if there are professionals on staff who can develop their ideas and administer the large introductory courses. This, in turn, depends on financial support by the college and the university.

Since survival of the University of Michigan chemistry curriculum depends on individual decisions made by faculty, administrators, and students, Ege says there is no way to predict the outcome with any certainty. After just two cycles, however, there is already some evidence that structure and reactivity is succeeding in attracting new students. The increase in sign-ups for the chemistry major is one indicator (fourteen to eighteen students per year in contrast with one to four per year over the five years preceding the introduction of the new curriculum). The number of students admitted to summer research programs, some of them to NSF Research Experiences for Undergraduates Sites, is another sign of success (they are doing very well, holding their own with older undergraduate and even graduate students). General interest in chemistry is a third indicator. When the department's research faculty gave presentations at an evening symposium hosted by the local ACS student affiliate last year, more than seventy students turned out. Faculty members report they are being overwhelmed by student requests to work with them in research.

Conclusion

Since 1988, Ege says, she has done little but "shepherd" curriculum reform aided by Brian Coppola who has also spent an "inordinate amount of time on it."

> I cannot begin to tell you how much time . . . went into the change here, mainly because my efforts are all mixed up with being chair of the curriculum committee, associate chair of

> the department, designer and teacher of the course over
> several terms, interpreter to other departments, and writer of
> changes in college bulletins.

As already mentioned, all of this was done with minimum external funding until the program was well under way. Not much internal support was provided either, except for start-up equipment funds available only because a new building was constructed. While the organic chemists carried the load the first three years, by fall 1992 Ege expects to have some inorganic chemists teaching structure and reactivity both to make sure that its content remains based on the important concepts of structural chemistry and to ease the burden on the organic chemists.

How to make change? Ege thinks she has learned a great deal about the process from the events of the past several years.

> Innovation is not a fix, but an ongoing negotiation of small
> changes, some of which work, some of which disappear. It
> requires a constant vigilance on the part of somebody who
> talks a lot, persuades a little, sets an example, creates an
> opening for others to be creative, and keeps on prodding and
> pulling.

For Ege, reform is very much a human endeavor.

Propagation

What is the likelihood that the long-term process which characterized the grass-roots reform of the chemistry curriculum at Michigan can be propagated? This question led me to the University of Utah where, in the course of my inquiries into freshman chemistry, I was told that some members were developing a modification of the Ege model. After Associate Chair Richard Steiner heard her talk at an ACS meeting, the curriculum review committee (chaired by William Epstein) solicited materials from Ege. I was curious both as to what had motivated the decision to revise the chemistry curriculum at Utah, and how the committee in charge was proceeding.

Curriculum reform at Utah began in 1989 when Peter Stang, newly appointed chair, charged the Undergraduate Education Committee to review the undergraduate program. Because of feedback from other departments, duplication of course content, deficiencies in the upper-division offerings, and a desire to establish objectives for lower-division revisions, curriculum reform was done in a top-to-bottom fashion.

The lower-division curriculum revision effort at Utah was fostered by a growing concern that 25 percent of the students enrolled in the first quarter of general chemistry failed to register for the second, and that the number of chemistry majors was falling (from forty-seven per graduating class in 1977 to as few as nineteen in the late 1980s). Revision was undertaken to reverse this trend and to prepare students for the revitalized upper-division courses. The Ege model appeared to be a good starting point for developing a curriculum that would accomplish these goals. However, after numerous brown bag lunches with all interested faculty, it became apparent that blanket transplantation of the Michigan curriculum was not warranted.

Instead, the faculty instructed the committee to develop a new introductory course sequence which reflected both the pedagogical interests of the faculty and exciting new areas of chemistry, while reducing the amount of mathematics required in the first year. By delaying the math component until the second year, the committee hoped to give first-year students a year to catch up. Topics in organic chemistry, they believed (as did Ege), could achieve all these goals. The committee then set itself the task of refashioning the existing six-quarter, single-track chemistry sequence by mixing and matching topics from the first two years. This sequence, they hoped, would provide students with a gentler introduction to, and more success with, college-level chemistry. It also allowed for more depth of discussion in quarters five and six of material peripherally covered in normal first-year courses. Unlike the Michigan program, the curriculum at Utah maintains one quarter of "introductory chemistry" before beginning organic chemistry. (See Appendix B, page 178 for a detailed description of the sequence.)

It was not hard to mix and match, reports Steiner, because the committee was "working toward a common goal instead of protecting individual turf." Faculty input was solicited through brown bag lunches, and regular committee reports were made to the faculty. As a result of faculty input, the committee decided to introduce the curriculum as a 125-student experiment beginning in fall of 1992. With one exception, the faculty unanimously endorsed the proposed sequence and the topic content of each course. After three years the experiment will be evaluated and a final decision made.

A social scientist cannot help but find it interesting that, although Utah's efforts were inspired by Michigan's, the program and the process by which it is being implemented are quite different. The model works at Michigan because a dedicated group of faculty made it work. An equally dedicated group of faculty at Utah has similar goals, but because of the expertise available there, the personality of the individuals, and a different, but equally justifiable approach to teaching chemistry, it has chosen a modified version. The point is that no model can be effective unless faculty trust it. And to trust it, they may have to reinvent the model at their own institution, with their own method of generating overall support. *This is what grass-roots reform is all about.*

5

"Not More Help, but More Chemistry"
UCSD's Approach to Nonscience Majors

What can be done to improve recruitment to science by way of introductory courses in college? This is the question that brought me to the door of Barbara Sawrey, lecturer in chemistry and academic coordinator of undergraduate chemistry at the University of California, San Diego (UCSD). UCSD's new courses are attractive if you start from my premise that real change in college science occurs at the individual program level, and that real commitment is measured by departmental initiatives and support. Chemistry 11, 12, 13 ("chem 11") is worth examining because of its nature, history, and because one of its creators and its senior instructor holds an unusual dual position: permanent lecturer and academic administrator. Most important, Barbara Sawrey's positions put her smack in the center of instructional and institutional change.

Take the history of chem 11 as one example. It was introduced in 1988 when overpopulated chem 4, one of the standard introductory offerings for majors and nonmajors alike, ran out of lab space. From the beginning, chem 11 was intended not to replicate chem 4, but to be a rigorous non-lab, three-quarter introductory sequence for a group of UCSD students diverse in background and in their interest in science.

For some UCSD students, chem 11 is one way to meet a year-long science requirement in certain UCSD colleges. The youngest of the UC campuses, UCSD is divided into five colleges, each with its own admission and graduation requirements, as a way of countering the vast size of a 20,000-student multiversity. UCSD students must take one to three quarters of science, depending on their goals. Some who take chem 11 could meet their requirements with an assortment of one-quarter biology courses, such as the very popular (1,500 enrollees) course in the biology of nutrition. But they choose chemistry instead, which suggests that they have positive memories of high school chemistry and that they are not afraid of the rigorous mathematical content of college level science.

In addition to students meeting a distribution requirement, chem 11 includes a few declared majors, among them transfer students from community colleges who find it useful or necessary to review introductory chemistry. Others find their way into chem 11 because professors of politics or business suggest it as a basis for environmental politics or law. The relatively small size of the two lecture sections, 350 in one and 150 in the other, may also be a factor for those who don't like large lectures.

Barbara Sawrey, who holds a doctorate in chemistry and worked in industry before returning to graduate school, interprets her appointment at UCSD as that of "instructional troubleshooter."[1] And, indeed, she is. In addition to teaching assistant (TA) training and overseeing the laboratory storeroom staff, any teaching she does is technically voluntary. Since her job includes coordinating general chemistry courses and lower division curricular revision, it was appropriate that, once identified, the population problem in chem 4 was hers to solve. She and the department's vice chair for undergraduate affairs recommended a course without a lab, a three-quarter introduction to chemistry, then moved on to what might be called the "R&D:" designing and teaching the prototype of chem 11 until it could be taken over by a colleague.

I met her in the third year of chem 11, when she was establishing a special section for potential chemistry converts. She invited me to attend some classes, have a rapporteur monitor the course and the special section, and interview her on how she is nurturing student interest in chemistry by means of chem 11.

What interested me was that this one course combines a "general education" in chemistry with a rigorous foundation. Given the nature of the course and Barbara Sawrey's reputation as a teacher, one could imagine that if you were going to stalk students capable of doing science anywhere in the university, chem 11 would be fertile hunting ground. As more colleges and universities institute general education requirements in science, shouldn't more effort be made to recruit nonmajors to science within the context of introductory courses? What can we learn from Sawrey's strategies that can be transferred elsewhere?

---

[1] Gabriele Wienhausen is Sawrey's counterpart in biology at the same rank of lecturer, with particular responsibility for biology laboratories. The University of California system, with its provision for permanent lecturers, has a number of persons in similar positions on other campuses. Sawrey calculates that there are more than thirty people with positions analogous to hers in chemistry at different colleges and universities around the country. Their salaries range from $16,000-$64,000 and their number is increasing.

The Course in General: What's in a Name?

What I noticed after auditing several meetings of the first quarter of chem 11 was that the course is packaged to attract the not yet committed. Instead of "introduction to general and inorganic chemistry," the chemistry department gave the three quarters provocative titles. Although coverage is far more standard than they suggest, the titles are a clever marketing device. Quarter one is called "the periodic table;" quarter two, "molecules and reactions;" and quarter three, "the chemistry of life." These titles are advertisements for chemistry, and Sawrey is not averse to employing such devices.

But the titles are the thematic underpinnings of the material as well as advertising. In "the periodic table," for example, students read the first eight chapters of a standard text[2] and do a great deal of standard chemistry, but along the way they explore with their instructor earlier versions of the periodic table. How the pattern and periodicity of the elements became known, and how chemists were able to arrange known elements and to predict new ones even before the quantum mechanical explanation for their sequence was understood, provides not only course subject matter, but much of its drama. Further, the theme permits Sawrey to incorporate some history of experimental and theoretical chemistry, and gives students an idea of modeling in science. In the second quarter, "molecules and reactions," she extends her discussion of the fundamental processes of chemistry. Appealing to students' interest in biology and environmental issues, quarter three addresses "the chemistry (biochemistry) of life."

As Sawrey intends it, chem 11 is a tour of chemistry in place of a foundations course. Students who complete the entire sequence emerge with more information about organic chemistry and biochemistry than those taking the standard version, but at the expense of some inorganic chemistry and certain basic procedures and skills. Yet Sawrey believes that if a student can be enticed into chemistry by way of chem 11, that student can be mainstreamed into the standard chemistry sequence with a one- or two-quarter bridge course. As academic coordinator she is committed to offering such a bridge for chem 11 students who change their minds about science, particularly if they switch during quarter one.

What Sawrey confronts is a fundamental contradiction in science courses for nonmajors: these courses are usually terminal. Should a student discover a certain talent for "general science," the only option is to become a specialist. Where are the upper level courses in general

---

[2] Robert J. Ouellette, *Introduction to General, Organic, and Biological Chemistry*, 2nd ed. (N.Y.: MacMillan, 1988).

science? While we must recruit atypical students in the standard introductory science course, we must also recruit them from the science
courses for nonmajors. A forgiving but uncompromising curriculum is
what Sawrey is attempting.

The Lecture Method

I sat in on a few lectures in the fall quarter of 1990 and made my own
observations. The instructor treats topics seriously, which makes her
students feel that they are learning real chemistry. Second, I noticed that
the instructor makes a strong effort to repeat major points and provide
breathing space for excursions into the history and applications of
various discoveries. Hers is a spiral and recursive lecture style. Explanations precede demonstrations and then are repeated after the demonstration has sunk in. The instructor adjusts her topics to respond to questions,
whether on environmental issues or why baking at higher altitudes takes
more time and less flour. She uses the chalkboard, transparencies, and
counter demonstrations. Her personal style is warm and reassuring.

Students enrolled in chem 11 select one of two large lecture sections
which meet three mornings per week.[3] There are no labs, but students are
invited to attend voluntary problem-solving sessions run by TAs who
also correct homework. One additional voluntary section was offered in
the fall of 1990 for students who wanted, as Sawrey put it, "not more help
but more chemistry." Rapporteur Suzan Potuznik, then a postdoc in
bioinorganic chemistry, now an assistant professor of chemistry at the
University of San Diego, monitored this noncredit special topics section
for this project. The question: Would students who elected special topics
be more likely to switch to chemistry as a major?[4]

The Students

On the basis of standard variables, neither the students who enrolled
in the fall of 1990 nor those in the special topics sections were promising
as converts to science. While 82 percent (300 out of 367) had taken
chemistry in high school and 61 percent (225 out of 367) had studied
calculus, the fact that they were not taking chem 6a, the standard

---

[3] Sawrey's coinstructor was not interviewed or observed for this chapter.

[4] During the next quarter Sawrey herself taught the special topics section and her
coinstructor taught the lecture course. Because of different requirements, college by
college, quarter two enrolled a total of about 250, and quarter three about 150, a considerable drop-off from quarter one.

introductory course, suggested (and a special topics questionnaire documented) that their hearts were elsewhere. When asked about prospective majors on their questionnaires, they listed literature, history, political science, psychology, and communications as favorites. Only fourteen were undecided and, except for forty-five who chose economics, most were not planning to go into math or math-based subjects. Indeed, of the nearly one-third who were taking math (to meet graduation or major requirements), about fifty-seven or half were in "elements of mathematical analysis," an introduction to calculus. When the TA asked students about science as a career during the special section, sixteen out of thirty said "not for me," and two responded with "yuck."

Sawrey had fully expected that a special kind of "quarter-one" student might elect the special topics sections and she recruited one of her best TAs to teach it. He was Stephen Everse, a graduate student in biochemistry and known on campus as a dedicated teacher. Everse was, as rapporteur Suzan Potuznik noted, a gifted and enthusiastic TA.

Still, those attending had mixed motivations for seeking "not more help, but more chemistry." On Everse's questionnaire, sixteen said that they had chosen special topics because its meeting times were convenient. Only eight wanted more than basics, three listed "real-world issues," and four said it sounded interesting. One enrolled, he said, because special topics sounded cool, and another because the section represented a change. Despite the label as a special topics section, students did want help on quizzes, but they were also looking for more. A few said they had come to learn why science is important, others to focus on the basics but in more depth, to learn about chemistry in real life, and to get to know other students. What they liked most about the section when it was over was their TA, and that sessions were interesting.

As in all experiments in higher education, Sawrey could no more predict the results than she could determine in advance who would sign up for the special section. All she could do was compare the performance of the students in the special topics sections and those taking help sessions, and then see who enrolled in chem 12 and 13. Sawrey anticipated that as many as sixty of the 367 students enrolled in her large lecture section would choose special topics sections. When a course is new, there is no student scuttlebutt, positive or negative to bias the outcome; sixty students did indeed sign up.

Sawrey's instructions to Stephen Everse were to not preselect topics but to let them emerge from student interests. In other words, he was to navigate the section rather than plan it. So no topics were announced, but interested students initially could assume, since this was chemistry, that the subjects would include environmental degradation, AIDS, nutrition, and the like. And, in fact, those were among the topics they chose.

After asking the students for comments, Everse divided the ten weekly sections as follows: orientation; a review session midway in the quarter; and, in the last week, thought-provoking questions prepared by Everse and the other TAs to help students prepare for the final. The remaining seven weeks were devoted to special topics, with some initial discussion each week about previous or upcoming quizzes.

The seven topics that emerged were: (1) Everse's own graduate research on fibrinogen; (2) AIDS; (3) nutrition; (4) drugs and the brain; (5) environment and pollution; (6) plastics, waste, and recycling; and (7) the ozone layer. At no time were the topics coordinated with the lecture material. The students didn't seem to mind this, according to rapporteur Suzan Potuznik, and, indeed, they were as interested and enthusiastic about controversial topics in chemistry as they were about politics. They were particularly responsive to anything Everse could share with them about his own and the wider world of research.

The Special Section

What do students who are not especially committed to chemistry want to know about the subject? What does an instructor offer them when they attend a section voluntarily? Everse had no firm curriculum, but he did have an agenda. His purpose was to seduce his students into chemistry by demonstrating his own enthusiasm for the subject, and by explaining in depth chemical effects important in everyday life. To get them involved he began by sharing his own doctoral research on fibrinogen. Since the question, "what is fibrinogen?" failed to evoke a completely satisfactory response, the discussion devolved to "what is fibrin and what are blood clots?" As the class got into the subject, Everse presented examples that could be made sensible with a model system–the perfect opportunity to talk about models and how a scientist chooses a model system and alters its parameters to make it possible to observe effects in a shorter time frame.

Everse displayed a test tube of fibrinogen and thrombin which polymerized to form fibrin. As students examined the test tube they were encouraged to ask whatever questions came to their minds, and he spontaneously led them into related areas such as growing crystals and X-ray crystallography. Everse's bag of tricks included a string of Ping-Pong balls to help his students visualize the polymerization and folding of fibrinogen, and he concluded with a discussion of the "snowball effect," how one chemical event starts a whole series of reactions. With fibrin, he made students understand that the challenge is to find at what point the clot formation sequence begins and can be stopped.

Everse's students were better informed about AIDS and knew such terms as "HIV" and "retrovirus," but their lack of chemistry, he helped them see, limited their ability to analyze the disease. A flow diagram of the immune system was Everse's introduction to killer cells, neutrophils, and macrophages, and he presented their function in simplified form before turning to anti-AIDS drugs and the challenge of finding a vaccine. Here students brought up social and moral issues (should prisoners be used for AIDS vaccine testing, for example). At the close Everse deftly brought the discussion back to biochemistry.

In the hour dedicated to nutrition the leading questions were what are nutrients, and how are they absorbed in the body? High and low density lipoproteins and "good" and "bad" cholesterol were familiar terms, but not their biochemistry. Everse next explained steroids and vitamins, asking leading questions with no penalties for wrong answers. Gradually the function of steroids, why some vitamins are water soluble and others fat soluble, and the sources of body energy became clear.

The following week the discussion turned to the brain and drugs. Students were liveliest when talking about drugs and drug abuse in terms of their own experiences with work-related testing. The brain structure, the brain-blood barrier, the function of the neurotransmitter and how its rate of response is affected by drugs were Everse's topics. Determined to focus on chemistry, he was able to return to the periodic table by mentioning lithium as a treatment for manic depression. Tackling cancer and the environment (the subject of another session), Everse first defined mutagens, carcinogens, and teratagens and why mutating cells divide rapidly. This led to a discussion of the chemical treatment of cancer and how anticancer drugs are designed to be tumor-specific.

The session on plastics and recycling began with composition (monomer polymerization), and Everse impressed upon students how many thousands of monomers are involved. Once he had the students thinking at the molecular level, he explained how plastics vary in decomposition, making them appreciate why recycled materials are generally thicker than standard forms. Solid waste, students were surprised to discover, is primarily paper and only 9 percent metals, 8 percent glass, and 7 percent plastic. Always returning to chemistry, Everse had the students speculate what temperatures would be necessary to kill bacteria and which plastics could survive such heating during recycling.

Earth's stratospheric ozone envelope, students needed to know, protects us from ultraviolet radiation. The ozone molecule absorbs high-energy ultraviolet light generating molecular oxygen and oxygen radicals. Chlorofluorocarbons generate chlorine radicals, which also react with ozone in the upper atmosphere. Although they were not familiar with radical chemistry, students could follow the reaction and the role of chlorofluorocarbons in atmospheric ozone depletion.

Suzan Potuznik, in monitoring Everse's special sections for this report, found his students to be far more involved than students in introductory chemistry, a subject she had often taught during her graduate years. Still, she noticed that few students were very active and many not active at all. There was a shyness about answering questions that required knowledge of which they were unsure. Potuznik observed that these students, many of them humanities and social science majors, were comfortable with discussion, but uncertain about the language of chemistry and "insufficiently practiced" in the logic of scientific deduction. The exercise of precisely those skills was another purpose of the special section.

Although there is no way of knowing how many chem 11 students were recruited to chemistry, their responses to a final questionnaire were heartening: fourteen said they would willingly take another chemistry course if it were structured like the first quarter. Five said "maybe," and at least as important, fifteen had "changed their mind" about science and scientists and felt more positive about both.

Conclusion

Barbara Sawrey's experiment proved inconclusive the first time around. Only one of the students from the special section went on in chemistry specifically because of it. Perhaps two or three more might have decided to do so after another quarter. It is this last that Sawrey ponders when she thinks about chem 11. For certain populations, she believes, chem 11 will be an important *alternative* route into chemistry. Among them: transfer students from community colleges; students who received inadequate or no exposure to the physical sciences in high school; and those interested in chemistry-based careers, but not confident enough to enroll in the regular chemistry sequence.

Suzan Potuznik thinks more majors could be recruited if UCSD's registration system were more flexible. It is difficult for freshmen to switch plans the same year, and anyone wishing to cross over to mainstream chemistry after chem 11 has difficulty negotiating the system. Even selection of the special topics section was hard for students because of university-wide scheduling rules. Another factor, Potuznik says, is counseling. If advisers let students wait until their last two years to fulfill science requirements, recruitment opportunities are lost.

Measured by student satisfaction, chem 11 succeeds but not, Sawrey believes, solely because of her teaching. The structure of the course, the fact that it presumes no prior knowledge of chemistry, and that it provides substantive links between topics make it special. "The TAs always say they learned about certain aspects of chemistry for the first time in this course," says Sawrey. This is true to some extent of all courses and all first-time teachers, but the sequence of topics and the sloweddown pace in chem 11, believes Sawrey, helps the TAs deepen their understanding.

The absence of laboratories in chem 11 leaves substantial gaps in students' hands-on experience with chemistry. Sawrey would gladly add laboratories to the course if places and equipment were available, but chem 11 was designed so there would be lab space for would-be majors. So, for the foreseeable future, the alternative has been to make chemistry come alive through in-lecture demonstrations.

Who will decide the future of chem 11? Barbara Sawrey is not obligated to teach it, but she is in a position to maintain it through her persuasive ability and influence over the teaching allocation process in the UCSD chemistry department. And since all students enroll voluntarily, that is, are free to take other courses to meet science requirements, their satisfaction with chem 11 (87 percent recommend the course, 92 percent the instructor)[5] is significant in the department's plans for the future.

---

[5] From UCSD's CAPE (Course and Professor Evaluations) booklet. Even when there was a different instructor in chem 11 in 1990 (recommended only by 61 percent of the student respondents), 83 percent still recommended the course.

Can Introductory Science Be Multidisciplinary?
Harvard's Chem-Phys

6

Because chem 11 was an attractive alternative to chem 4 at UCSD, Barbara Sawrey had a ready-made demand for the course. Dudley Herschbach and David Layzer, laboring to launch a new, integrated chemistry-physics course at Harvard, did not. That proved to be a major problem.

Chemistry 8-9 ("chem-phys") resulted from a confluence of good intentions. Conceived by three Harvard scientists, it was meant to satisfy three different but complementary agendas. Biologist John Dowling wanted to accelerate and make more meaningful chemistry and physics training of "future physicians."[1] His idea was to combine first-year physics and general chemistry in a two-semester course leading to organic and biochemistry. These, in turn, would provide a solid foundation for a third-year course in molecular and cellular biology.[2]

Chemist Dudley Herschbach was looking for an approach to general chemistry that would encompass the physical basis of modern chemistry–primarily twentieth century atomic physics. The traditional physics course treats mainly Newtonian mechanics, leaving students of chemistry to make their own connections to thermodynamics and atomic structure. David Layzer, the third member of the team, professor of astrophysics and a popular instructor in Harvard's core curriculum, wanted a new approach to introductory physics with more reading and writing. Once the kinks were out, he hoped chem-phys would became a core course that would attract nonscience majors.

---

[1] At Harvard, where 98 percent of all students who apply to medical school are accepted, the term "future physician" is preferred to the term "premed."

[2] The medical school deans (Daniel Tostensen and Gerald Foster) were particularly anxious to provide undergraduates with the kind of introduction to science that would prepare them for the "new pathway" method of teaching medicine at Harvard.

Thus with a small grant from Harvard's former president, Derek Bok, moral support from the medical school dean and from David Pilbeam, associate dean for undergraduate education, and with the active support of mathematician Daniel Goroff, chem-phys was born.

The course omitted some first-year physics topics–sound, optics, dynamics of rigid bodies, and special relativity–to address atoms, molecules, crystals, quantum theory, and statistical thermodynamics. Subject matter was further constrained by three additional requirements: depth, self-sufficiency, and coherence. "Difficult but important concepts like the covalent bond and the second law of thermodynamics will be fully developed, from the ground up, in ways . . . intelligible to students with a limited mathematical background," reads a course handout.[3] Most of all, the course designers wanted to tell a connected story on the ground that, as Layzer expressed it, "the human mind is better equipped to understand and remember stories than to memorize encyclopedias."

Since the team's goals were far more ambitious than those of standard first-year physics or chemistry courses, they would not be able to use a standard course format with lectures, problem sets, and problem-solving sections. Instead they decided to adapt the format of Layzer's core courses on "space, time, and motion," and "chance, necessity, and order." As in the core courses, two reading and writing assignments for weekly discussion sessions substituted for lectures and problem sets. Students could progress at different rates according to their knowledge of science, and course grades would assess performance in light of each student's background. Even more unusual, reading assignments would be drawn mostly from primary sources, such as the writings of Lavoisier on conversion of mass, from Bohr's theory of the hydrogen atom, and from Einstein's quantum theory of radiation. Selections from Carnot's *Treatise* would be discussed, for example, in terms of its contribution to the theory of thermodynamics, despite Carnot's incorrect assumption that heat is a conserved quality.

Since there were no sources that treated topics the right way at the right level, Layzer prepared notes to supplement existing materials, a much larger project than anticipated. Unit I, "The Atomic Hypothesis," begins with the following overview.[4]

> Everyone knows that the formula for water is H_2O and that Columbus reached America in 1492. But the grounds for these two beliefs differ radically. The second belief rests on

---

[3] All descriptions of the topics of the course are paraphrased or taken verbatim from David Layzer's handout, "About Chemistry 8-9," prepared for the course in 1989.

[4] From chem 8-9 course material prepared by David Layzer.

historical documents. The first is supported by a complex web of inference and experiment. In this unit we will reconstruct that web.

The unit continues with an unusual introduction to the kinetic theory of gases. First, there is the "idealized mathematical model of a gas which will supply statistical interpretations of two macroscopic physical quantities, temperature and pressure, and will predict a relation between the pressure, the temperature, the volume, and the number of molecules in a sample of ideal gas." Then the historical evolution of current theory is described.

Throughout this first unit (and subsequent ones) there is frequent mention of themes and of the way scientific knowledge accrues. There is, for example, an explanation of the subtle and complex relationships between "qualitative empirical generalizations, quantitative empirical rules, theories, hypotheses, and conjectures," and how, above all, macrophysics and microphysics are linked. Assumptions are described as just that (e.g., "the frequency distribution of molecular velocities in a gas is isotropic"); and their justifications (e.g., statistical entropy) are foreshadowed. This approach is in stark contrast to standard courses in which physical concepts follow one another without any sense of where the course or the professor is headed.[5]

Unit one is an ambitious 100-page chapter covering molecular velocities and collisions; the origin of gas pressure, force, and momentum; the limitations of the ideal gas law; molecular formulas and atomic weight; electrons, electronic charge, and the atomic nucleus; the ordering of elements; mass and energy, and conservation of matter and energy. Throughout, key formulas are mathematically derived (presuming some familiarity with multivariate calculus), and the whole is explained against a background of the history of thought and discovery. For those who can follow the argument, the web is finely woven.

What were Herschbach's and Layzer's students supposed to *do* with all of this? First of all, read. Then prepare essay answers to a problem set with questions calling for "explanation and discussion." These assignments, in turn, were read by instructor Ruben Puentedura, a senior TA, and returned within a week with suggestions for revision. The assignment received a "structured discussion" during two ninety-minute sessions each week after which it was assumed students *understood* everything they had read.

---

[5] See the author's *They're Not Dumb, They're Different: Stalking the Second Tier* (Tucson, Ariz.: Research Corporation, 1990) for comments by students on the problems with the standard introductory course in physics, passim.

In making sense of each unit, Layzer expected his students to "improve their problem-solving, writing, and discussion skills, and their ability to read and understand scientific and mathematical texts."[6] The lab part of the course–some assignments involving the computer–helped make theoretical subject matter concrete, gave students basic laboratory skills, and taught experimental problem solving. Grading was done on the basis of successfully completed assignments.

After several months of meetings and substantial work by Layzer in the summer of 1989 (preparing handouts and writing the first four units), chem-phys was offered to Harvard-Radcliffe undergraduates for the first time in the fall of 1989.

Problems surfaced immediately. The core committee rejected the course because of its prerequisites. Students were expected to have taken advanced placement chemistry, physics, and calculus in high school to qualify for chem-phys. This, the committee argued, contradicted the spirit of the core.[7] The chemistry department (Herschbach's home base) approved chem-phys as the equivalent of a one-semester introduction to general chemistry, but physics would not follow suit. This meant that Harvard's "future physicians" could not be sure how chem-phys would count in their medical school applications.

Partly because of the foregoing and partly because of poor course advertising, only two sections of chem-phys filled, each with fewer than ten students, the first time the course was offered. The poor enrollment was surprising given student complaints about Harvard's traditional introductory science courses.[8] Some of the seventeen students who did enroll enjoyed and learned from the course, but all had a hard time. The handcrafted material was more mathematically demanding (and more demanding of literary skills) than either Layzer or the students had anticipated, and he simplified the material for the second year. Now, said the course handout, "the mathematical language of the narrative and of the assignments is carefully graded like steps cut into the side of a mountain, and every important . . . concept is discussed anew in its scientific context."[9] But the word along the grapevine, a source students trust more than the catalog description, was that "you have to be a mathematical genius to do chem-phys."

---

[6] David Layzer, "About Chemistry 8-9."

[7] The core curriculum at Harvard takes the place of general education requirements elsewhere.

[8] Personal communication from Abigail Lipson, Bureau of Harvard Study Counsel. See infra for more of Lipson's assessment.

[9] David Layzer, "About Chemistry 8-9."

Although it was expected that fifty students would enroll by the second year, only seven brave souls registered for chem-phys. They entered a much-revised course with better text, less rigorous math, and more experienced teachers. A visit to the class in fall 1990 found students remarkably responsive to the material and to the Socratic dialogue TA Puentedura led them through. But it was clear that, although the course met the goals of its designers, chem-phys might ultimately not make it at Harvard.

The Promise of Chem-Phys

The course designers had written extensively about the differences between chem-phys and the standard courses and how intellectually rewarding it would be, but its special nature was not well communicated. If students did not already know how interesting chem-phys promised to be, they would never have guessed from the catalog description.[10] Once a student ventured into the first class, a more detailed course description, which underscored chem-phys differences and benefits, awaited. Also appealing, given the typically large lecture classes at Harvard, would have been the opportunity to learn science in small class discussions. But by the time this became known to other students, it was too late to enroll.

Another feature of chem-phys was ample feedback: in a course with exams but no curve, students were graded on the *quality* of their written work (the two weekly assignments plus twelve lab reports) and the *quality* of their contributions to classroom discussion. The short turn-around time for assignments to be read would permit instructors to "tailor each meeting to the needs of the group, and to monitor the progress of individual students." In addition to regular class meetings a third section was scheduled on Fridays for individual conferences and small-group meetings.

In design, chem-phys was intended to meet student objections to standard introductory courses: small class size; individual attention; cooperation among students; flexible syllabus that could be tailored as required; opportunities to pursue interesting questions in physics and chemistry in some depth; and a chance for students to demonstrate, orally and in writing, their understanding of a concept.

---

[10] By fall of 1990, without Department of Physics approval, chem-phys had to be called officially chemistry 8 and chemistry 9. It was described in Harvard's 1990-1991 *Courses of Instruction* as an "integrated, self-contained introduction to atomic and molecular structure, chemical thermodynamics, and chemical kinetics," and was not listed as fulfilling any requirements.

The Experiment in Pedagogy

Chem-phys was more than an innovative course, at least for Herschbach and Layzer. It was an experiment in an alternate pedagogy as revealed by, if not the catalog description, a great deal of material on "how to take this course." Abigail Lipson, a clinical and cognitive psychologist at the Bureau of Harvard Study Counsel and supervisor of our student rapporteurs, digested all the material produced by course designers and summarized what made chem-phys pedagogically interesting.

In contrast to an introductory course organized around bite-sized segments of new material, Lipson notes, each chem-phys unit began with a complex phenomenon which was then teased apart, an approach mirroring scientific inquiry. Further, chem-phys students were to question the material presented and make their own judgments. The content was to be learned in context rather than in isolation. Layzer made these differences explicit in his handout on how to approach reading and writing assignments.[11]

> While you are learning physics and chemistry, you will also be learning to learn. Your central objective should be to build up a repertoire of thoroughly understood and usable concepts, theories, and techniques. Whenever you are reading, writing, talking, or thinking about a topic connected with the course you should have that objective in mind.

In the traditional model, students are given new material piecemeal, but once learned they may not return to a unit for a long time. In chem-phys concepts were revisited more than once and from more than one angle. Lipson calls this "multiple exposures;" Arnold Arons, "reiteration."[12] In his handouts, Layzer frequently returned to the analogy of a *repertoire*. Like musicians, the students were to know certain pieces so well that they could "perform" them at a moment's notice. Nevertheless, they should regularly revisit them to deepen their understanding and polish that performance. They were to combine concepts, theories, and techniques *as they were learning them* to form a coherent, well-integrated whole.

Also noteworthy in chem-phys was the willingness of instructors to address "why" questions. Instead of being told when a principle is and is not applicable, students were asked to challenge, speculate, predict, test, explain, and justify its applicability and its limits. They were to tap into what they knew, identify what they didn't know, and keep an eye on

---

[11] David Layzer, "About Chemistry 8-9," p. 40.

[12] Arnold Arons, *A Guide to Introductory Physics Teaching* (New York: John Wiley and Sons, 1990).

the "big picture." This was not incidental to the course. In his 1990 essay, "Chem 8-9: A New Approach," Layzer ascribes the "distorted picture most students have of math and science" to standard introductory courses and texts that discourage "why" questions and pay little attention to unifying concepts.

The "Academic Bends"

Despite the promise of chem-phys, the goals were more difficult to realize than either professors or students had realized. Simply stated, the new pedagogy took getting used to. Layzer and Herschbach called this the "academic bends:" students had to adjust to greater "depths" and different demands. Students reported some or all of the following problems: (1) not knowing how to cope with questions they didn't immediately understand; (2) not knowing how to cope with problems involving multistep solutions; (3) not knowing what they were supposed to be getting out of discussions.

Katya Fels and Steven Brenner took chem-phys the first year it was offered. Katya returned as an undergraduate teaching assistant–Steve was hired to be one, too, but enrollment fell too low–and both went on to take organic chemistry the following year. Since they were familiar with the course and able to judge its value as students of organic chemistry, they were well qualified as on-site rapporteurs.[13] Their assessments of student difficulties are similar to Lipson's. One was the students' need for more certain content. Even occasional lectures would have given students a framework on which to hang concepts. A second problem was the instructors' assumption that chem-phys students would be able to pick up a great deal on their own. Katya thinks the course designers overestimated students' ability to master one set of difficult concepts and go on to the next.

> If someone is trying to do electric potential problems without really understanding what a potential is, the problem takes on a new level of complexity, a totally unwelcome one. . . . Professor Layzer assumed that we were already at that level where we could pick up new subjects just by being told the concepts.

Neither the course designers nor TA Puentedura appeared to have realistically estimated how much time coursework would require. Puentedura thought that the weekly problem assignment would take

---

[13] In addition, Chris Lowry, a high school science teacher, served informally as a reader of the various materials generated by the project and contributed many insightful comments.

about three hours, the reading about one. Katya and Steve, in contrast, put the problem assignment at six hours (not more because "people give up after six hours"), and the reading at three to four.[14] Chem-phys class discussion did not achieve its intended goals, and students very often came unprepared and did not get much from one another. More serious was the students' unmet need, as Katya and Steve recall it, for "raw information" (in contrast, traditional courses are criticized for covering too much without developing students' capacities to discover, evaluate, and use the material). Discussion proved, in their view, "a particularly unhelpful medium for straightforward information gathering." As a possible solution to this problem Katya suggests, almost reluctantly, that perhaps what chem-phys needed was "something like a lecture," exactly what the course designers had wanted most to eliminate.

Returning to chem-phys a year later, however, Katya observed that students were able to recall formulas without having memorized them because they wrote and talked so much about their underlying concepts in class.

The Mathematics Component

Layzer and Herschbach felt very strongly that mathematics should be employed as a *language* in chem-phys and not as a mere collection of formulas and algorithms.[15] Daniel Goroff, a member of the Department of Mathematics and of the Derek Bok Center for Teaching and Learning, joined in the effort to unify physics, chemistry, and mathematics. During the first year Goroff led special sessions on mathematical topics. Despite this care, the mathematics embedded in the unit narratives provided the basis for the rumor that chem-phys required "a mathematical genius." The level of math was lowered and the amount of work reduced the second time around. More important, efforts were made in the second year, both in Goroff's sessions and in the course itself, to help students learn how to *use* mathematics. Also by the second year the sequence of topics was revised so that the mathematical topics came in the "right order and with the right spacing." For 1992-1993, the mathematics department, chaired by Wilfried Schmid, has agreed to offer two new courses in advanced calculus closely coordinated with chem-phys. Taught by Daniel Goroff and using the same reading-writing-discussion

---

[14] Steve comments that these estimates come from the second year. In the first, he found himself spending fifteen hours per week on chem-phys and often not completing the assignment even in that amount of time.

[15] David Layzer, "Chem 8-9: A New Approach," 1990.

format as chem-phys, the new math courses will allow students to explore the mathematical ideas and techniques of chem-phys in greater depth and breadth. (See Appendix C, page 179, for the new integrated course sequence.)

The lessons from the first year produced many improvements in course materials, but revision continues. As Layzer says, the course is being composed "with a word processor, not a chisel." And he is grateful for criticisms and suggestions.

What Chem-Phys Accomplished

I. "Real" Problem Solving

While much remains to be done, chem-phys did achieve some stunning results among students who were ready for it. Katya liked the fact that science as inquiry was a focus of the course, that she was taught how to think and how to incorporate new knowledge with old. Best of all she felt that introduction of new topics by way of a narrative demonstrated that "going off on a sidetrack is neither wrong nor irreversible;" that "science isn't just something one knows, it is something one does." Watching how different people engage the same complex problem in different ways made science "come alive," a contrast to the stultifying effect of standard textbooks.

The emphasis on writing out one's ideas in longhand rather than in the cryptic language of symbolic mathematics revealed students' learning styles. One classmate, Katya reported, wrote "wonderful essays . . . always presenting the larger picture. . . . She was very good at determining where large, basic flaws in the problems lay, the assumptions behind other students' presentations, and the logical consequences if these assumptions happened not to be true." A senior in computer science took a different approach. He was very quantitative, insightful, "nitpicky," and sometimes rigid. "It was very interesting," Katya writes, "for everyone, students and instructors alike, to watch the two interact in class."

What students gained from these discussions, Katya thinks, is that "problem solving inherently involves a lot of struggling, puzzling, trial and error, false starts, and dead ends." And this was news, she believes, to many who had never engaged in extremely difficult problem solving before. Katya contrasts these efforts with what she calls "rote problem solving" where "either you get the right answer or you've forgotten the formula." She thinks students in chem-phys learned that there are times when science is very difficult, and the best thing to do is subdivide the problem until it becomes a series of approachable subproblems. As she puts it, this turns the impossible into the "excruciatingly difficult," but also makes it possible to begin to work.

> When a scientist sets out to solve a [real problem in science] he or she doesn't wait for divine inspiration. He writes down what he knows, tries to manipulate and analyze this, sees what next step has to be taken, and then works backward from there.

She also believes that the rough drafts expected of students were a refreshing change from the idea (conveyed in other science courses) that "you have just one chance to get the answer right." "Real chemists and physicists," she learned in this class, "spend a lot of time working in circles, trashing what they've done and starting again, and getting wrong answers." She also discovered that scientists do not work in isolation. "Though it's important to be able to think on your own, it is also important to work with other people, to assist and to critique their work." It is easy to see how students might have initially felt uncomfortable with the open-endedness, uncertainty, and frustrations they encountered in what Katya calls "real problem solving." But they ultimately came to appreciate these as part of the very nature of scientific inquiry, even to recognize that "science is a lot more creative than people give it credit for."

II. Challenging Authority

Another theme that appears throughout Katya's and Steve's journals concerns authority. Even in deliberately student-friendly, noncompetitive settings, students tend to defer to the teacher's authority. Katya herself, a confident and willing learner, never asks a question in her organic chemistry course. "It's not that I don't have any. I feel that a question has to be insightful or brilliant, the discovery of something new, something my professors and section leaders have [never heard] before. So [instead of asking it] I tend to go home and try to figure it out for myself." Even in chem-phys, which featured discussion, there were "long, long silences." Students remained mistrustful and fearful of authority. The elimination of the grading curve, the small group format, the patience of the instructors–none of these succeeded, at least initially, in making students feel safe enough to participate freely without fear of evaluation or failure.

But by the end of the course our rapporteurs believed chem-phys had positively affected participants' willingness to challenge authority and to assess independently their own performance. The fact that Layzer and Herschbach often joined the class, "dissipating" authority in Katya's words, made a difference. When Katya, an undergraduate peer of the students, was engaged the second year as course assistant, authority was dissipated still more. Students reserved their "dumb questions" for her and honed their skills disagreeing with her.

Yet another factor in mitigating authority was the course's unwavering commitment to the idea that knowledge is constructed by human beings and that scientific "facts" are not written in stone. If scientific models are fallible, then so might be science texts and even science professors. This is very different from what Katya and Steve call the "I know all the answers and you are here to learn them from me" approach, in which professors position themselves, as Steve expresses it, as the "repositories of all knowledge." What Steve gained from chem-phys was a certain irreverence. "The course taught me that professors don't know everything, even about their own subject." Speaking up in class, engaging his professors, challenging givens, and tackling hard questions are the skills he feels were nurtured in chem-phys. When he moved on to organic chemistry, he found himself

> . . . more aggressive with the material, challenging every statement, questioning every source; [also] diving deeper into problems; wanting to know not just empirical facts but how and why things are the way they are. I also find myself trying to generalize my knowledge to see what it is that I really know. I try to form my own conceptual model . . . and occasionally put it into writing.

Both Katya and Steve again experienced the "academic bends" upon "surfacing" to return to standard courses. Katya reports feeling gypped in organic chemistry, but not really sure why. "Perhaps it's because the course material is presented in such a way that it seems deceptively logical: 'here's the rule for this and here's a list of exceptions,'" she speculates. She and Steve also miss the close relations between students and instructor in chem-phys. One of Katya's professors in another course did invite the class to ask questions immediately after class. But for Katya this was not much use. "Who really has questions right after class? It usually takes a couple of days for things to click or not." Besides, she felt that the professor was expecting questions of clarification, not about basic concepts.

They miss the collaboration and discussion. The isolation of the traditional course is harder than before for them to tolerate. Most of all, they miss the "real problems" that engaged them in chem-phys.

> The problems [we work on in organic chemistry] use only a small set of concepts and don't require any "leaps of faith" or great insights. If you're smart and knowledgeable, you can do them fairly easily. In chem-phys the concepts were less

> evident and required [group] brainstorming and trial and
> error for the hard points, and the problems were large enough
> that they could be broken up to work on the smaller ones.
> While my problem sets this year are more accessible, they are
> proportionally less rewarding. . . . I don't feel I've achieved
> anything once I'm done.

By the end of the semester immediately following Steve's graduation from chem-phys, he was feeling a combination of sadness and nostalgia for the course. He found himself not "questioning the material in organic chemistry" and felt that "the material was becoming just a chore, no longer challenging me." Then, at the end of the semester, he came across a problem on the final take-home problem set which was "not obvious." Two different textbooks had different formulas for the same value. Why?

> It was not really necessary to answer this question because
> from the handout it was clear what [the professor] wanted.
> But I wanted to know why this discrepancy existed. I spent an
> hour working. Eventually I gave up and called Katya. . . . I
> could not think of anyone else who wouldn't just say "the
> answer is so and so" and not care about the discrepancy.

Together, out of their own curiosity and interest, Steve and Katya figured out the source of the discrepancy. Katya had shared with Steve the experience of chem-phys where, as Steve remembers, they had often been given conflicting information and assigned the task of making sense of it. This gave them, they think, a real understanding of how to approach science.

Analysis

Chem-phys is designed to be taught in small classes and features discussion and contact with the instructor. It encourages depth of understanding rather than breadth of coverage. Students "chunk" newly acquired knowledge by making connections between and within theories and between abstract ideas and the physical world, rather than merely memorizing facts. Further, chem-phys is graded to make it noncompetitive, and encourages group work and collaboration. It was created precisely to avoid the pitfalls and solve the problems that plague many traditional science courses. Beyond this, it was designed to demonstrate an alternative science pedagogy.

So what went wrong? Where are all the students? Why aren't they beating down the doors to enroll in chem-phys? In addition to being hard, the course seems to have run aground on institutional barriers. It is as if, in Trotsky's fateful words, "You can't have socialism in one country."

Unless more than a single course is changed, real reform of science cannot take place even in a single institution.

The first problem to surface, as Abigail Lipson underscores from her perspective as a Harvard adviser,[16] was the question of credit: how does chem-phys count in the Harvard system?[17] As a year of physics? A year of chemistry? A half-year of each? Is it similar enough to other chemistry and physics courses that it can meet the requirements of other departments? Or, is it so dissimilar that it should be taken *in addition* to them? And how will the course "count," not just at Harvard, but in the larger academic and professional worlds—premed, for example.

Some of these questions have been settled, but not all. Chem-phys does not fit neatly into the slots of the larger Harvard and other postgraduate systems. It is not equivalent to any other existing course—a testament to its truly innovative nature. Almost a year after completing it, both Katya and Steve were still arguing with their departments about how chem-phys should be counted on their transcripts. Until the problems are resolved, many students are understandably reluctant to spend a quarter of a year's schedule (and perhaps half of their personal time) on a course that may not satisfy their requirements. This is especially true at Harvard where students are expected to complete undergraduate work at the rate of four courses per semester for eight semesters. They must specifically petition to work at a different rate or to take a ninth semester in residence. Every year the college worries about the departure of a few students and "lost degrees," those who fail to complete credit requirements in the allotted time. Students who are balancing course schedules to complete the core, departmental, freshman year, and perhaps premed requirements, need to know exactly how chem-phys will count. And the course needs to fit into busy schedules that may contain electives as well as required courses.

Another issue is marketing, and not just marketing to students. "We should have enlisted wider support in other departments at the outset," Layzer now concedes. Students learn about courses from the faculty and in other ways, but few faculty were familiar with chem-phys. The catalog

---

[16] What follows is taken pretty much verbatim from Abigail Lipson's own analysis in her final paper for this project of what went wrong with chem-phys.

[17] A not too dissimilar effort to combine chemistry and physics in a single course, established at the University of Wisconsin-Green Bay in the early 1960s, foundered on just such a problem. Since students wishing to transfer to the University of Wisconsin at Madison were unsure how their version of chem-phys would count, the course had to be abandoned. See C.R. Rhyner, J.C. Norman and F.A. Fischbach, "The Chemistry-Physics Program at the University of Wisconsin-Green Bay," *American Journal of Physics*, 42, December 1974, pp. 1106-1111.

description didn't explain its nature and said only that "the course meets entirely in sections." The course designers meant to communicate that chem-phys is conducted as a seminar, but at Harvard, professors give lectures, and "sections" are usually led by graduate students. Hence, the course description may have conveyed wrongly to students that "You'll never meet a real professor in this course."

A third factor is the course's reputation. Word was out almost immediately after chem-phys was offered that this course was no cakewalk. Steve speculates that, faced with choosing between a gut course with "terrible ratings" and one with rave reviews requiring twenty hours a week of hard work, most students, even serious students, will choose the gut.

There are several reasons for this. Students probably recognize that, with small-group discussion meetings, they won't be able to shirk homework, not even for one class. Students with multiple long-term commitments, at Harvard and elsewhere, meet them all only by short-term juggling. Any course that provides little leeway for work rate variability is less attractive. The course is also one in which students are expected to make sense of difficult material on their own. For students insecure about their intellectual abilities or who fear evaluation (and that includes most students, even at Harvard, Lipson says), the exposure may be too threatening. "It was threatening," Steve confirms, "but it was surviving that let us become more self-reliant."

Student perceptions are something of a catch-22 for a course designed to foster independent scientific thinking. Students more comfortable with formulas and problem sets may be unwilling to take it. A result may be that chem-phys will only teach to the "converted," attracting students who already value the chem-phys approach, but not those who might benefit from it most. If chem-phys aims at reform rather than simply providing an alternative for motivated students, then the present "take it if you can stand it or leave it" policy is very much off the mark.

What's Ahead for Chem-Phys?

Dudley Herschbach was much less involved than David Layzer in constructing the course and overseeing its day-to-day operation, but he remains a firm believer in the course's value as an alternate introduction to chemistry. In answer to my question about the failure of chem-phys to enroll more students, he replied that the course was severely handicapped by not winning course approval from the physics department. Without physics' imprimatur, the concerns of Harvard's "future physicians" could not be allayed. The fact that both Ruben Puentedura and

David Layzer were selected *by students* for the prestigious Phi Beta Kappa Teaching Award at Harvard the second year that chem-phys was offered indicates, Herschbach believes, that students appreciated the quality of the course and its pedagogy. As this is being written, however, the mood in physics is changing. Howard Georgi, department chairman, is enthusiastic about a chem-phys sequence enlarged to include parallel courses in mathematics. While his department has (so far) only agreed to list chem-phys as "related," and will count the course in meeting only certain requirements, mathematics is now firmly committed to providing a mathematics complement for each semester of chem-phys. Layzer and Herschbach intend to market the course more aggressively in 1992-1993. They will inform all freshman advisers in a more structured way, and will try to better match student ability with course expectations. The new catalog descriptions feature the multidisciplinary nature of what is now a four-semester sequence in mathematics, physics, and chemistry, with applications to biology. (See Appendix C, page 179, for the new catalog entries.)

Looking ahead, Herschbach fears that even if chem-phys survives (and for a while in 1990-91 this was not certain), finding instructors to teach the course will not be easy. Puentedura is an advanced student of chemistry with a strong background in physics and an understanding of both disciplines that far exceeds the norm. "No one," says Herschbach, "has ever *taken* courses like this one. How will they know how to teach one?" He might have added that since even good students, the kind Harvard recruits, haven't had courses like chem-phys, they may not know how to take one.

Meanwhile, chem-phys has begun to demonstrate some of the shortcomings in the way elementary physics, chemistry, and mathematics are conventionally taught and learned at Harvard. "Some people who were (and are) skeptical of chem-phys are discovering that their students don't understand *their* lectures and demonstrations or the point of their problem sets, either." The chem-phys group is more convinced than ever that it is on the right track.

The key, says Layzer, is time–time to get a course into shape, time to build a supportive consensus among colleagues for the new venture. Chem-phys' staying power, however fragile, allowed the course to evolve. It is now very different from what was originally conceived. Materials have been changed, assignments have been altered, there is now a mathematics component the course designers had not at first thought to include. "Curriculum reformers," concludes Layzer, "cannot simply take the position that they have something to sell. We also have very much to learn."

7
Reforming College Physics
Attending to Cognitive Issues

More than in other areas of college-level science, reformers in physics are asking not only what ought to be the content or sequence of physics courses, but what do we want our students to know? What do we want our students to be able to do when they complete our courses?[1]

As a result of this focus, few college-level physics programs have been overhauled in the manner that Trinity and the University of Michigan have revamped their chemistry offerings. Instead, a number of researchers, including physicists, cognitive psychologists, specialists in artificial intelligence, and physics educators have been trying to create a knowledge base on which radical change can be built and justified. For the physics community, then, the question "what works?" is less a matter of creating programs to recruit, instruct, and retain students (though some programs do a fine job) than discovering what works best, first theoretically, then practically, as curricular and instructional strategies.

The advantage of this approach is that it corresponds to the way science proceeds and scientists work–it is familiar, comfortable, and, though often dependent on outside funding, not necessarily limited to local conditions or local support. One disadvantage is that it takes a great deal of time to see what the bits and pieces of research add up to, and to guide textbook publishers and instructors in translating new findings into classroom practice.

It is difficult to predict where physics education is heading, and whether or not we are on the brink of major, sustainable reform. Textbook publishers seem to think we are. Nervous that their standard texts will be left behind, they are signing on as authors or editors critics and innovators whose ideas would have been considered radical five years ago. At every meeting of the American Association of Physics Teachers (AAPT) there are twenty or more presentations on cognitive issues in

---

[1] See Arnold Arons, *A Guide to Introductory Physics Teaching* (New York: John Wiley and Sons, 1990).

teaching and learning physics. Even the research-oriented American Physical Society (APS) recently featured major plenary sessions on the subject, and has just established a new "Forum on Education" boasting nearly 1,000 members. Heated discussions on pedagogy, content, instructional technologies, and problem solving travel at the speed of light by E-mail and along Bitnet. But introductory physics courses are still so standardized that four texts dominate 90 percent of the market. The physics community is trying to combat this standardization by removing certain topics as part of the "less is more" strategy; and by adding new topics so that introductory courses reflect current research in modern physics.[2] But if there is to be long-lasting change in undergraduate physics, there is a long, hard road ahead.

Because such a large fraction of the physics community wants to do "theory-based curriculum design," an outline of their studies of cognition prefaces a summary of three exemplary programs in undergraduate physics.

Studies of Cognition

Conceptions and Misconceptions

For many years, the physics community has been uncertain about how college students–even good students–reason about the material in introductory physics. One line of research has pursued alternate conceptions (so-called misconceptions) which, researchers believe, go far to account for students' inability to *qualitatively* understand physical processes. Lillian McDermott, professor of physics at the University of Washington, has written widely on student perceptions of kinematics, dynamics, optics, and electric circuits; she has also conducted experiments and interviews documenting students' misconceptions in mechanics, and has proposed some solutions.[3] At the University of Massachusetts, Jose Mestre and colleagues are working on computer-based methods to help students perform qualitative analysis of problems based

---

[2] Introductory University Physics Project (IUPP), sponsored by the American Physical Society and the American Association of Physics Teachers, is dealing with just these questions. See also the proceedings of an NSF-sponsored conference on teaching modern physics in "Quarks, Quasars, and Quandaries," ed. G. Aubrecht (College Park, Md.: American Association of Physics Teachers, 1987), and a new text by Jonathan E. Reichert, *A Modern Introduction to Mechanics* (Englewood Cliffs, N.J.: Prentice Hall, 1991) in which classical mechanics is preceded by substantial phenomenology of particle physics.

[3] L.C. McDermott, "Research on Conceptual Understanding in Mechanics," *Physics Today*, 37 (7), (1984), pp. 24-32; "Millikan Lecture 1990: What We Teach and What is Learned–Closing the Gap," *American Journal of Physics*, 59, (1991) p. 301.

on scientific principles.[4] Fred Goldberg, head of a new research center and graduate program in mathematics and science learning at San Diego State University, is studying student perceptions and misperceptions of physical optics.[5] And Richard Hake, at Indiana University, is focusing on overcoming barriers to understanding Newton's laws of motion.[6] Where the misconceptions field was once inhabited by a few widely dispersed researchers, it is now crowded with projects here and abroad. A glance at the citation index shows that, as of 1991, there are more than 800 articles in refereed journals on misconceptions in physics.

Much of the interest in misconceptions derives from instructor experience with the *persistence of naive conceptions* that students bring with them to introductory physics. These misconceptions were always present, but until recently were presumed to be temporary since it was thought that a brief exposure to dynamics, for example, would suffice to replace naive notions about motion with the Newtonian view. Long ago Arnold Arons, now professor emeritus of physics at the University of Washington, commented that many students who complete the first-year program in physics remain "Aristotelian" in their views of motion. But it was not until 1985 when David Hestenes and Ibrahim Abou Halloun provided a convincing experimental demonstration of the "failure of conventional [college-level] instruction in physics to overcome students' naive misconceptions about motion"[7] that the physics community as a whole took note. Hestenes and Halloun designed a test to measure students' qualitative understanding of the physical principles underlying Newtonian mechanics and gave it to 1,000 students about to enroll in introductory physics, then to those who successfully completed the course. The results showed only a "very small gain in understanding"

---

[4] See "Enhancing Higher-Order Thinking Skills in Physics" to be published in *Enhancing Thinking Skills in the Sciences and Mathematics,* ed. D. Halpern (Hillsdale, N.J.: Lawrence Erlbaum, in press).

[5] F. Goldberg and L.C. McDermott, "An Investigation of Student Understanding of the Real Image Formed by a Converging Lens or Concave Mirror," *American Journal of Physics, 55,* (1987), pp. 108-119.

[6] See Richard R. Hake, "Promoting Student Crossover to the Newtonian World," *American Journal of Physics, 55,* (1987) pp. 878-884 and John Clement, "Students' Preconceptions in Introductory Mechanics," *American Journal of Physics, 50,* (1982) pp. 66-71.

[7] See I. Halloun and D. Hestenes, "The Initial Knowledge State of College Physics Students," and "Common Sense Concepts About Motion," both published in *American Journal of Physics, 53,* (1985), pp. 1043-1055 and 1056-1065. See also D. Hestenes, M. Wells, and G. Swackhamer, "Force Concept Inventory," and D. Hestenes and M. Wells, "A Mechanics Baseline Test," published together in *The Physics Teacher, 30,* March 1992, pp. 141-158 and 159-166. These new papers contain updated findings and measures for evaluating and categorizing students' misconceptions in mechanics.

and, even more significant, that this "small gain" was independent of the instructor.

Much of the research into misconceptions and many of the alternate pedagogies being developed are intended to address such results. Instead of presenting the "scientific view" and expecting students automatically to substitute it for their misconceptions, these pedagogies are designed to activate specific misconceptions, cause students to feel uncomfortable with their previous ideas, and from this discomfort (sometimes called disequilibration) to have them deliberately *construct* new knowledge. This means that the physics instructor is to respect students' deeply ingrained ideas, develop teaching strategies that call forth less *memory* and more *thinking* about real-world problems and, most radical of all, seek to be not so much a repository of knowledge as, rather, "present at the birth of new ideas."

Novice to Expert Problem-Solving Strategies

Another problem in cognition is that most introductory physics students, even the better ones, do not progress from novice to expert in problem-solving techniques, regardless of teachers or textbooks. The first task of research on the problem has been to analyze and demonstrate the *differences* between novice and expert.[8] The second has been to see if the experts' problem-solving method is transferable to novice students.[9] Fred Reif, Jill Larkin, and others have shown that experts approach physics problems in the context of their physical environments, and depend very much on qualitative representations. Novices begin at what is for experts the last step–identifying the equation for a particular problem. They rarely think about the problems either physically or in terms of *type*. Mestre and others at the University of Massachusetts, Amherst are exploring how computers might be used to teach students this sort of expert problem-solving behavior.[10]

While instructors are quick to recognize these failings, they are not nearly as sure as researcher-innovators how to test and teach more appropriate problem-solving strategies. So long as physics students can pass examinations by means of "plug-and-chug," there is little incentive–

---

[8] Jill H. Larkin, John McDermott, Dorothea Simon, and Herbert A. Simon, "Expert and Novice Performance in Solving Physics Problems," *Science, 208*, (1980), pp. 1135-1342. See also F. Reif and J.I. Heller, "Knowledge Structure and Problem Solving in Physics," *Educational Psychology, 17*, (1982), pp. 102-127.

[9] F. Reif, "Teaching Problem Solving–A Scientific Approach," *Physics Teacher, 19*, (1981), pp. 310-316.

[10] See "Enhancing Higher-Order Thinking Skills in Physics," *Enhancing Thinking Skills . . .*

except among the dedicated–to master harder, more time-consuming methods. It is possible to render examinations more open-ended to test for deeper comprehension, but few large departments believe they can afford the necessary staff time to grade short explanations and written comments.

Ordering New Knowledge

The third issue for physics educators is how courses (and, as a result, students) organize physical knowledge. Conventional instruction appears to students like building different rooms of a house, one room at a time. First the foundation, walls, roof, plumbing, and wiring are completed for one room; then everything is repeated for the next. But while physicists understand that the principles used to build the "mechanics room" apply to all others (up to relativity), conventionally taught students rarely grasp this. This was demonstrated by researchers who took forty problems from a standard textbook, put them on cards, shuffled them, and asked students to group the problems by type.[11] Experts worked from fundamental principles, sorting problems by "dynamics," "work-energy," and "momentum conservation." Students, however, unable to see fundamental similarities, grouped by surface features: inclined planes problems, spring problems, rope problems. One professor employing this test at a community college (David Wright) reported that he even got a pile of "hinge problems."

How this research contributes to reform in college physics is the question that brought me to examine reforms in the making at New Mexico State University, Dickinson College, and Case Western Reserve.

Overview Case Study Method—New Mexico State

While David Hestenes and Ibrahim Halloun were showing that students who pass introductory physics do not have a qualitative understanding of the subject matter (in Hake's terms, "do not cross over into the Newtonian world"), New Mexico State's Alan Van Heuvelen was attempting to correct this same deficiency in a large lecture course.

Professor of physics Van Heuvelen had been following research reported in the literature and at APS and AAPT meetings, and was familiar with the cognitive problems reported in physics. In 1985, Arthur

---

[11] M.T.H. Chi, P. J. Feltovich, and R. Glaser, "Categorization and Representation of Physics Problems by Experts and Novices," *Cognitive Science*, 5, (1981), pp. 121-152. See also Arnold B. Arons, "Student Patterns of Thinking and Reasoning," Parts 1-3, *Physics Teacher*, 21, (1983), pp. 5766-581; 22 (1984), pp. 21-26; 22 (1984), pp. 88-93.

Farmer, a physics teacher at Gunn High School in Palo Alto, California, wrote about an "overview case study" (OCS) approach to teaching in *The Physics Teacher*. The three-part system attracted Van Heuvelen because it meshed with what the physics community was learning about cognition. The "overview" portion of the lesson let the instructor focus on conceptual issues. During a middle "exposition" part, students learned to represent concepts mathematically, thereby modeling expert problem-solving strategies. Finally the "case study" gave students an opportunity to apply what they had learned to an advanced problem involving more than one physical principle.

Adapting and enlarging on Farmer's material, Van Heuvelen first taught a college version of overview case studies in 1987. "I had been teaching for more than twenty years, giving 'great lectures,' but had never before really known what the students were thinking," he remembers. Instead of lecturing on Newton's three laws of motion he had students observe a number of experiments on an air track and come up with their own principles. "It didn't take long for them to suggest experiments or to challenge my statements and interpretations of events." Students and teacher were hooked.

Since 1987 Van Heuvelen has been writing materials for the OCS approach, using them, testing students on the qualitative and quantitative aspects of introductory physics, and comparing their scores on the Hestenes-Halloun test to those of conventionally taught students. He has also been giving workshops around the country, and collaborating with others on projects of mutual interest. Along the way he has spent two fall semesters with David Hestenes at Arizona State University on an NSF-funded project, and has won a grant to author materials for wider distribution.[12] Van Heuvelen claims that the more OCS resources he has at his disposal the less he lectures, and the less he lectures the more his students learn.

OCS in Action

When I visit his campus I find Van Heuvelen teaching a typical calculus-based physics course. His 140 undergraduates, most of them engineering majors, are still using the standard text. But he has also given them an "active learning" study guide which explains that the course is organized around "conceptual chunks," each with the same sets of activities. The overview part of OCS in Van Heuvelen's version includes the representation of physical quantities in terms of diagrams and

---

[12] Called ALPS–Active Learning Physics Sheets–and available from their author, c/o Department of Physics, New Mexico State University, Las Cruces, N. Mex. 88003.

graphs; small-group discussion of basic principles; and the analysis of physical processes without computation.[13] Following the overview comes the exposition. Here the fundamental mathematical equations are introduced for the first time, and students are taught to solve problems using pictorial representations as well as formulas. But the overview sequence remains in force: students are first to go after qualitative understanding, then a mathematical treatment of the model, and finally to apply the model to the solution of problems.

The case study is a problem which requires students to draw knowledge from everything that has come before. A typical case study might employ kinematics, work-energy, projectile motion, and circular dynamics, all in one. What Van Heuvelen is trying to prevent is the "spring error"–the temptation to assume the relevant formula is the one last associated with a familiar object. Instead, his students are learning to identify not the *familiar*, but the *essential* in a problem. Throughout the course, handouts are available that remind the students where they've been and where they're going, how far the house they're building is from completion and, above all, how several fundamental principles are shared by different rooms.

What is unusual in this approach is: first, the focus on conceptual reasoning; second, that students are figuring out principles for themselves; and third, that pictorial representation is presented as a key step, whether in the free-body diagram in dynamics, or in the work-energy bar graph Van Heuvelen has invented to help analyze energy conservation. The point is to overcome students' previously learned habits of treating every physics problem like an applied mathematics problem.

Examinations have to be constructed and graded differently. In addition to standard problems, Van Heuvelen includes qualitative questions–sometimes in clusters–that test understanding of physical principles. He very often reverses problems, going from their mathematical representation to the physical situation from which they derive. He gives his students case studies to describe and certain carefully phrased multiple choice questions. The work of preparing and grading exams like these–following through a student's reasoning in solving complex nonstandard problems–requires time, time that a grant from the Fund for the Improvement of Post Secondary Education (FIPSE) from 1988 through 1991 has provided.[14] How such activity can be mainstreamed,

---

[13] A description of his course and its outcomes can be found in his articles, "Learning to Think Like a Physicist: A Review of Research-Based Instructional Strategies," and "Overview Case Study Physics," both *American Journal of Physics, 59,* October 1991, pp. 891-907.

[14] The Fund for the Improvement of Postsecondary Education is a division of the Department of Education.

without department-wide commitment to this new approach, is yet to be determined. Nonstandard examination types and questions can be circulated among physics faculty, but who will do careful, line-by-line grading?

Alan Van Heuvelen sees himself preparing students to do well on the type of qualitative posttest that conventionally taught students fail, and to do better on quantitative problem solving as well. "What makes this possible," he believes, "is having students construct concepts–rather than simply handing them predigested material–and an approach to problem solving that emphasizes *qualitative* thinking and pictorial representation." His course is now getting attention both inside and outside New Mexico State University. There are 100 copies of his carefully crafted materials in circulation and, perhaps even more significant, some of his colleagues at NMSU are using them.

Workshop Physics—Dickinson College

The private liberal arts colleges educate only a fraction of the nation's undergraduates, but together produce a disproportionate number of professional scientists (and mathematicians).[15] Recently the results of a two-year study of the science and mathematics programs of 200 liberal arts colleges and universities was published. Called "Project Kaleidoscope," it describes a number of successful programs at these institutions and includes recommendations for improvement elsewhere.[16] Our focus is on more typical, mainstream institutions, but there is one program in the Kaleidoscope survey that should be included in any discussion of what works in college level physics. Because of its radical departure from most approaches and its commitment to adapting to learning environments typically found at large universities,[17] workshop physics at Dickinson College deserves attention.

Workshop physics was begun in 1986 at Dickinson, a small liberal arts institution in central Pennsylvania, when it was found that physics students, despite small classes, individualized instruction, and an unusual computer-based laboratory program, were doing no better (actu-

---

[15] J.P. Gollub and N.B. Abraham, "Physics in the Colleges," *Physics Today*, June 1986, pp. 28-34.

[16] "What Works: Building Natural Science Communities," Project Kaleidoscope, 1991. Available from Project Kaleidoscope, 1730 Rhode Island Ave., N.W., Suite 1205-ICO, Washington, D.C. 20036.

[17] Taken from "Interactive Physics," proposal to the Fund for the Improvement of Postsecondary Education (FIPSE), 1989. A packet of materials, entitled "Workshop Physics," is available at no cost from Priscilla Laws, Department of Physics and Astronomy, Dickinson College, Carlisle, Penn. 17013.

ally a little worse) on the Hestenes-Halloun mechanics concept test than students elsewhere.[18] Despite high teacher ratings by students, a group of faculty concluded that this was a problem they couldn't ignore, and decided to make at least one radical change: abandon lectures in favor of a computer-enhanced workshop in introductory physics. In the words of proponent Priscilla Laws, professor of physics and astronomy, workshop physics is designed to teach by means of "guided inquiry rooted in real, concrete experiences . . . from which students are to *construct* their own knowledge of abstract principles."[19]

> Taking [conventional] introductory physics . . . is like trying to take a drink from a fire hose. There are far too many topics presented . . . too many abstract theories about things that don't constitute part of everyday reality. . . . The majority of students . . . do not have sufficient concrete experience with everyday phenomena to comprehend the mathematical representations of them.

Beginning in 1986, FIPSE awarded Laws and her team[20] grants now totaling $600,000 to develop workshop physics. FIPSE suggested that the Dickinson group collaborate with Ronald Thornton and colleagues at Tufts University Center for the Teaching of Science and Mathematics on the use of microcomputers as laboratory instruments. During the first year of the grant, the Dickinson group continued to use the lecture method while they tested, polled, and interviewed students in introductory physics. Their students were not unhappy with the way physics was taught, Laws reports, but they had two complaints about the introductory courses:[21]

> . . . that attending lecture and lab sessions did not leave enough time [for their instructors] to teach them problem solving, and [that there was] a lack of connection between lab activities and lectures. Laboratories seemed superfluous because they did not help students master the textbook problem-solving skills needed to get good grades. The narrow understanding of what it means to know physics, which we had communicated to students via our traditional teaching methods, was at odds with the new goals we had developed.

---

[18] "Workshop Physics: Learning Introductory Physics by Doing It," *Change,* July / August 1991, 20-27; "Calculus-Based Physics Without Lectures," *Physics Today, 24,* (12), 1991, pp. 24-31.

[19] Taken from an invited talk by Priscilla Laws at The Conference on Computers in Physics Instruction, North Carolina State University, August 1, 1988.

[20] The team includes John Leutzelschwab, Robert Boyle, and Neil Wolf from Dickinson.

[21] Laws, "Workshop Physics . . .," p. 22.

After finding funds to remodel laboratory facilities and outfit them with Macintosh computers, the team spent the summer of 1987 developing student activity guides for both algebra- and calculus-based courses. These guides are workbooks for students to enter predictions, observations, develop theories, and apply them to quantitative experiments. By fall of 1987 all was ready to offer workshop physics for the first time.

A preliminary step was to reduce course content by 30 percent. Then the team removed all formal lectures, replacing them with sections of twenty-four students meeting for three two-hour workshops a week. Each section had one instructor and two undergraduate teaching assistants, who staffed labs during evening and weekend hours.[22] Pairs of students shared a computer, an extensive collection of scientific apparatus and other gadgets. Among other things students pitched baseballs, whacked bowling balls with rubber hammers, pulled objects up inclined planes, attempted pirouettes, built electronic circuits, ignited paper with compressed gas, and devised engine cycles using rubber bands.

What remains of the standard two-semester introductory course is included in the student activity guide in twenty-eight units on selected topics. The guide, which is keyed to the textbooks,[23] provides exposition, questions, and instructions, as well as blank spaces for student data, calculations, and reflections. The unit-week begins with a pretest of students' preconceptions and invites them to make observations. After discussion the instructor helps them develop definitions and mathematical theories. The week usually ends with quantitative experimentation designed to verify mathematical theory.[24]

The computer is used extensively, but not in the usual computer-assisted instruction. Programming is de-emphasized because, as Laws writes, "previous attempts to include it in the introductory lab left us using physics to teach computing rather than the other way around." Instead, the decision was made to employ the spreadsheet as the major tool for calculation.[25]

---

[22] With a total enrollment of seventy-five students, the allocation of faculty contact hours is essentially the same as it had been under the lecture system at Dickinson. But at other universities, with much larger lecture courses, this would not be the case. Additional students were hired to help with classroom discussion and equipment management.

[23] D. Halliday and R. Resnick, *Fundamentals of Physics*, 3rd ed. (New York: Wiley, 1988); R. Serway, *Physics for Scientists and Engineers*, 2nd ed. (Philadelphia: Saunders, 1986); J. Faughn and R. Serway, *College Physics* (Philadelphia: Saunders, 1986).

[24] The above description is taken from Priscilla Laws' invited talk at the Conference on Computers in Physics Instruction, cited above.

[25] See R. Thornton, "Tools for Scientific Thinking–Microcomputer-Based Laboratories for Physics Teaching," *Physics Education* (22), 1978. See also Charles Misner and Patrick Cooney, *Spreadsheet Physics* (Reading, Mass.: Addison Wesley, 1991).

Dickinson's computer-based laboratory has three purposes.[26] First, computers display a real-time graph of changes in physical variables such as position or temperature. This helps students develop an intuitive feeling for graphs and for the phenomena they are observing. Second, students enter data directly into a spreadsheet for analysis and eventual graphing. Spreadsheet calculations become a tool for numerical problem solving and mathematical modeling. Finally, the use of a real-time raw plot helps students discover for themselves how to use physical definitions in the measurement of, for example, velocity and acceleration. Where acquiring real data is not feasible or is too time-consuming, students can use simulations for a ball rolling down a set of inclined planes, for wave interference, or for the display of electric field lines from a collection of charges.[27]

Although computers play a large role in workshop physics at Dickinson, Laws insists that the focus is still on direct experience and that the program could survive without them. Still, much of what is tested relies on the kind of data generation and data analysis that is greatly facilitated by computers. Indeed, the two-hour exams students take every few weeks are not only twice as long as exams in more traditional courses, but feature sections on concepts, data analysis, and experimental design in addition to standard problem solving.

Since the fall of 1987 over 250 students have completed workshop physics courses under six different instructors. Although assessment is ongoing, Laws and her team identify gains in several areas:[28] (1) student attitudes toward the study of physics; (2) a 30 percent increase in enrollments in upper level physics courses at Dickinson (and a proportionate increase in majors); (3) better mastery of concepts difficult to teach because they involve classic misconceptions; (4) improved student performance in upper level physics courses and in solving textbook problems (as well or better than students in traditional courses); (5) greater experience working in laboratories and with computers; and (6) improved understanding of the observational basis of physics and the

---

[26] This section is taken from Priscilla Laws' "Workshop Physics" article as it appeared in *Change*, July/August 1991, p. 25.

[27] These software simulations have been developed, respectively, by David Trowbridge of Carnegie Mellon University, Eric Lane from the University of Iowa, and B. Cabrera, from the University of California, Santa Barbara.

[28] Priscilla Laws, "The Role of Science Education Research and Computers in Learning Without Formal Lectures," Pew Trust Symposium on Teaching Strategies in the Sciences, Cornell University, June 19, 1990, pp.15-18. See also P.W. Laws, "Workshop Physics: Replacing Lectures with Real Experience," *Conference on Computers in Physics Instruction*, E.F. Redish and J.S. Risley, eds., (Reading, Mass.: Addison Wesley, 1990).

connections between concepts. As part of an effort to test the transferability of workshop physics to other, larger universities, David Sokoloff of the University of Oregon has adapted Priscilla Laws' materials for 200 students in an algebra-based physics course which normally features a fairly traditional format–lectures and weekly laboratory sessions. The course lends itself to evaluation, since half of Sokoloff's students are *only* enrolled in the lecture portion of the course, while the other half attends lectures and laboratory sessions. Based on a force and motion diagnostic test developed by himself and Ron Thornton of Tufts, Sokoloff finds that the combination of interactive lecture demonstrations and laboratory "substantially increases conceptual learning and retention."

The Revitalization of Physics 125: Case Western Reserve

Five weeks into his honors introductory physics course at Case Western Reserve University in Cleveland, Robert Brown, institute professor of physics, distributes an anonymous questionnaire in order to find out from his class of 120 freshmen whether they have had enough access to him so far. One hundred percent of his class regularly answers "yes" to this particular item. "How is this possible?" Brown asks his interviewer impishly as if he were telling a riddle. His answer: "E-mail!"

For the past three years at Case Western, thanks to the university's installation of a fiber optics computer network in all undergraduate dormitories, Brown has been able to hold office hours, display homework hints, correct any mistakes or omissions in his thrice weekly lectures, and answer all students' questions almost immediately by means of a course-specific bulletin board system (BBS) to which his students have access on their home computers. Not only does he get instant feedback from one and all ("when a homework problem is confusing, I get a barrage of mail"), but students can confer with one another simply by logging into physics 125 from their dorm rooms.

Within five weeks they not only feel they know their instructor and one another better, but Brown has a feedback loop with which to fine-tune his lectures and assignments. By the time the questionnaire was distributed this last fall there were more than 100 entries on the bulletin board, all of which could be retrieved any time. Half of the entries were from the professor, the rest from students having to do with aspects of homework– "I think problem eleven violates the principle of energy conservation," says one–or with aspects of physics not covered in their introductory course which have come up in conversation or are in the news. For those who want to reach their professor in person, there are plenty of old-fashioned office hours.

"Imagine this," begins Brown, warming up to the tale he is about to tell of the revitalization of physics 125. "One hundred students sign up for the course at preregistration. Two weeks later after the drop and add period there are twenty more in class." Students interested in physics as a possible major are particularly welcomed, but so are premeds, engineers and, since Brown has taken over the course, "anyone with an earnest desire to get in." Females constitute about 20 percent of the enrollment, performing as well as males. With Brown's abolition of grading on a curve, over 50 percent of the students finish the two-semester course with an "A," and no one drops out.

What the addition of E-mail has done for physics 125, says Brown, is phenomenal. He can now cover the basic material in the standard physics text at twice the normal pace, allowing him to allocate one-third of class time to cutting-edge physics. For the past two years students have read Gleick's book, *Chaos*,[29] heard about Brown's own research in particle physics, and studied the greenhouse effect. In the spring semester, the students read Richard Feynman's *QED*.[30]

The reason Brown can cover so much is the interaction he maintains via the bulletin board. His three weekly homework assignments employ the material covered in class. Since students have access to him and to each other they waste little time spinning their wheels. Still, to allow time for new subject matter to be absorbed, he schedules one week of review before each of the three monthly exams and the one final that all students must take to pass the course.

Instead of limiting coverage of physics to " . . . the speed at which I can write on the blackboard," Brown passes out skeletal notes for each class, skeletal because there are blanks for attentive students to fill in. This saves time and precludes unintelligibility, since the key equations and diagrams are preprinted for reference and review.

Case Western makes long-term, interest-free loans to help undergraduates purchase the required computers (Mac or IBM-compatible 386 machines). Brown has purchased a Mac in addition to his PC so that he is compatible with all of his students. The 120 enrollees in physics 125 are listed in one file with their E-mail addresses. Brown has only to type in a message, call up the file, and send it to individual students or all at once. Students, in turn, are alerted that they have E-mail as soon as they turn on their machines.

"It's nice for students, embarking on homework, to find out how others are attacking a particular set of problems," says Brown. The fact

[29] James Gleick, *Chaos* (New York: Viking, 1987).

[30] Richard P. Feynman, *QED: The Strange Theory of Light and Matter* (Princeton, N.J.: Princeton University Press, 1985).

that grading is absolute and not on a curve contributes to the cooperative spirit of the class. Brown also thinks that not being forced to face him frees students to ask questions that would tax their ability to "speak physics" during direct contacts. For Brown, access to his students' problems and misconceptions has greatly improved his teaching. He now includes optional problems, "the hardest I can find, which I would not have been able to do as a freshman." Brown also asks short-essay exam questions that stretch student skills and comprehension.

Not surprisingly, most of the E-mail queries concern conceptual issues that surface when the student sits down to solve a particular problem set. Students may start out saying they know how to solve a problem using the equations they've been taught, but don't really know what "tension" (for example) is. E-mail not only encourages digging, but risk-taking. "Students can speculate wildly about a problem, knowing they will get feedback from the professor before the assignment is due," says Brown. He also benefits. "When a problem is poorly stated, I hear about it right away," he laughs.

The revitalization of introductory physics at Case Western began inauspiciously when the department chair asked Brown to consider taking over physics 125 in the fall of 1988. Brown had been doing frontier physics in his upper division courses and was considered a good teacher. Physics 125 wasn't in trouble–the previous teacher was excellent at what he was doing–but course content and enrollment were stagnant. The first year, Brown admits, was only ordinary. He offered the frontier physics segments, but found himself unable to give all the homework assignments he thought the students needed, and was unhappy with the average class performance. When the fiber optics network was added in late 1989, students started E-mailing him questions. He quickly got up to speed on the network and discovered its possibilities. It was an unstructured innovation as far as Brown was concerned: neither Case Western president Agnar Pytte nor Ray Neff, vice president for information systems, were definite about how the system would be used when they initiated it. But they were confident that faculty and students would find ways to use it, and they were right. Today Brown believes that networking with students will turn out to be a far more useful application of the computer to teaching than instructional software. He now gets more questions from more students in class than he ever did before.

Concepts and Conversation on E-Mail

To give me a sense of what student-professor and student-student interaction is like via E-mail, Brown gave me the unedited network correspondence for a single week during fall semester, 1991. I found myself sorting it into three categories: (1) questions related to problem sets that Brown may or may not have covered in class, but for which students needed further clarification and elaboration; (2) common conceptual confusions, including "wild" speculations that Brown now has a chance to deal with; and (3) feedback to (and from) the instructor about specific problems, about exams, about the course, and about physics generally. The batch of E-mail also included a couple of tales of woe, unrelated to physics, but very much to the late adolescent lives of physics students.

"I have a question about the problem with the plane traveling in a vertical circle and releasing a coin at the top of the circle," begins one missive. Trying to figure out the direction the coin will travel (perpendicular or tangential), the student is confused. This, a physicist tells me, is a very common confusion, having to do with reference frames. Brown might well have dealt with it in class, but it helps this particular student and the rest of the class reading the correspondence that Brown has a chance to clarify it by E-mail.

Sometimes student questions are specific, sometimes remote and speculative, the kinds of questions not likely to be asked in class, not even in the privacy of the office: "I was wondering, if time is just a fourth dimension, why is it not measured in meters, like the other three?" (The student was confusing physical coordinates with mathematical coordinates.) Often Brown will get a number of questions on a single topic (like tension or Newton's third law). When this occurs, he may direct a response to everyone in the class. Still, he makes it a rule to answer each student individually, sometimes quite personally–"Well, you are much further along than I was at your age," he writes to a student anxious about his abilities.

The style is informal. Students write the way they talk with "sort ofs" and "you knows" dotting their prose. Brown is more articulate but not stuffy. When asked specifically to go over something in an upcoming review session, he writes back, "okeydokey. Just raise your hand if I forget." Because they get to know their instructor better as a result of E-mail, some students feel comfortable asking personal questions. ". . . I am double majoring in physics and astronomy so I find that stuff [special lectures on cosmology] fun. How did you decide to teach physics? I would like to teach also . . . " What's missing from the E-mail (owing no doubt to the limitations of a particular word processing system) are graphics (no free-body diagrams show up on the screen) and complex mathematical equations (integrals, for example). On the other hand, this forces students to express in spoken language the physical ideas they are trying to grasp.

Even the best students enrolled in physics 125 cannot always get what they need to know out of lecture or their text. One writes: "I have already heard your explanation of [nonconstant forces], but I'm still not comfortable with it. The explanation in the book is [also] not enough. If you would please reply to this message and explain it one last time. . . " Nor are they able to sort out what is relevant and what is not in a particular physical situation. Responding to their questions by E-mail gives Brown the opportunity to repeat certain points and to draw students' attention to others.

Analysis

Laws and Van Heuvelen have obviously been influenced by physics education research. Both are at pains to have students observe and speculate prior to being given the "scientific view" of physical phenomena. Instead of denying student misconceptions as if these play no role in the process of learning physics, they seek to activate these so that students can consciously replace old meanings with new ones. Their employment of enhanced (more difficult) problems is intended to have students link concepts instead of mastering them in isolation–all of which contributes to students' ordering of new knowledge. Brown appears to be attempting the same, but in a less organized fashion, simply by exponentially increasing the frequency and depth of his two-way communication with the students in his class. E-mail allows Brown to examine what his students are thinking before, during, and after the presentation of new knowledge.

How are students responding to these improvements, and what is the chance that any can be exported? Laws and her colleagues have done the most extensive querying of students. While there are complaints that workshop physics is too complex and time consuming (six class hours per week plus six to eight hours outside class to complete activities and assignments), the new approach earns high ratings from nearly all of them by the end of the second semester. They enjoy being active and acquiring computer skills. Most important, when tested on mechanics concepts, workshop physics students show statistically significant gains over students in the standard course, having developed more than *procedural knowledge*.

Not all students are happy with the *perceived* increased work load. Even though the number of topics has been reduced, more different types of learning are required: textbook, problems, observations, experiments, discussions with peers, essays, mathematical derivations, data analysis, and the writing and revising of formal laboratory experiments. One subset of students (about 10 percent) state emphatically that they would prefer a return to the lecture format. These students resent having to "teach themselves everything"–a comment that Steve made in reflecting on why chem-phys at Harvard might not be popular (see chapter 6). Laws and her team take these criticisms seriously; they continue to try to simplify demands made on students and on themselves. They insist, however, that more physics students were unhappy with the traditional course than are frustrated with workshop physics.

But the question of exportability cannot be answered with surveys of student satisfaction at Dickinson. Can an inquiry-based approach to introductory physics as labor- and laboratory-intensive as this one be adapted to larger settings? A second grant from FIPSE is making it possible to test the workshop model not only at the University of Oregon, but at Boise State, Nebraska, Ohio State, and Rutgers. To extend the concept to other disciplines, mathematicians at Dickinson and elsewhere are working on a "workshop mathematics," and biologists at Dickinson have designed computer-interfaced experiments in physiology for their introductory course.

Priscilla Laws is an indefatigable disseminator. She appears at many science education conferences with a video of her students' responses to workshop physics and examples of the microcomputer-based laboratory tools her group is using. She is publishing widely, not just in physics education journals, but for a more general readership, as in *Change*.[31] Outside funding is making it possible for the project to offer information, sample materials, microcomputer-based laboratory software, and traveling workshops to all who are interested. The project has "propagation" written all over it. Still, workshop physics is expensive, both in terms of capital purchases and faculty time, and even Laws admits that "our enterprise is both exhilarating and exhausting."[32] Whether faculty elsewhere will be willing to give up lecturing, and whether graduate TAs will be willing to take on the tasks that undergraduate assistants are doing at a liberal arts college, remain to be seen.

Students are not complaining about work load at Case Western Reserve. But Brown might well. "The best thing about E-mail is that everyone is working more productively than ever, including me," says Brown. "As we speak [we are meeting at a conference in Racine, Wisconsin] my students are talking to each other about homework assignments ten and eleven which I typed in just before leaving Cleveland. When I get back, there will be questions and comments . . . . I look forward to that."

---

[31] Priscilla Laws, "Workshop Physics. . .," *Change*, July/August 1991, p. 27.

[32] Ibid.

He doesn't look forward quite as much to grading the first exam, which is one week away. Because of the short essay questions and problems that invite speculation, Brown reads all 120 examinations and grades them himself. It takes an entire weekend, from 5 P.M. Friday to 10 P.M. Sunday, but it's worth it, he thinks. It's the best way he knows, together with E-mail, to diminish the impersonal effects of the large class. In addition to an ever-improving grade point average, Brown thinks that the fact that twenty students stuck with physics until graduation this past year (compared to ten to fifteen in previous years) reflects the networking which began four years ago.

Propagation at Case Western is less intensive and extensive than at Dickinson. There are twenty-two faculty in the Department of Physics, over half involved in teaching introductory physics. Brown has not made any formal presentations to the department or to his colleagues in other science fields at Case. Nor has he written about or traveled to many meetings to tout his course improvement strategy. But there has been good local publicity about the homework networking. The physics faculty who teach core courses have become increasingly interested in E-mail, and are now beginning to put "homework hints" on the network for their own students.

Alan Van Heuvelen believes that the overview-case study method has wide applicability and that, in time, his active learning materials will be included with auxiliary items that accompany standard texts. He has been giving workshops around the country to physics instructors ranging from community college teachers to research university faculty. His publications generate so much mail that he has had to set up a post office box to keep it separate. So long as outside funding provides copying and postage, he is willing to mail out his materials to all who ask. But Brown and Van Heuvelen are still loners in their respective departments. And, while the times seem ripe for change, without additional injections of support–from funders or from the physics community more generally–even these successful programs may wither. Reform has not yet, except perhaps at Dickinson, involved structural change.

8
Students Teaching Students
Harvard Revisited

For physics instructors a first encounter with unexamined assumptions about teaching and learning a subject they know well can be just as "disequilibrating" as students' experiences trying to cross over from the Aristotelian into the Newtonian world. Eric Mazur, Gordon McKay Professor of Applied Physics at Harvard, knows this because in less than two years he has transformed himself from a successful lecturer to a determined reformer of introductory physics. It was a painful, sometimes depressing, but ultimately exhilarating task to rethink the standard approach, he says. Today he is both creator and publicist of an improved method of teaching large lecture courses.

Mazur had been teaching physics 11 for eight years–successfully, he thought, judging by student ratings and their performance on his standard exams until, in 1990, he came across Hestenes and Halloun's *Force Concept Inventory.*[1] Like many, Mazur's first response was "not *my* students." Still, he was challenged to see if the paper was right, and decided to present Hestenes and Halloun's test to 200 introductory physics students in his calculus-based course for premeds, engineers, and honors biology majors, and to 100 students from another physics course. While Harvard undergraduates did a little better than Hestenes and Halloun's average, fully 40 percent failed to extend quantitative problem-solving skills in mechanics to a qualitative understanding of Newton's three laws. Mazur writes:

> After a few months of physics instruction all students are able to recite Newton's third law–"action is reaction"–and most of them can apply this law to problems. . . . [But] when asked, for instance, to compare the forces in a collision between a heavy truck and a light car [a typical Hestenes-Halloun

---

[1] The Force Concept Inventory is a newer version of the Hestenes-Halloun test of qualitative understanding of mechanics. See earlier discussion, chap. 7, p. 98.

example], a large fraction . . . firmly believe that the heavy truck exerts a larger force on the light car than the reverse.[2]

The first warning came when he gave the test to his own class and a student asked, "Professor Mazur, how should I answer these questions? According to what you taught us, or by the way I *think* about these things?" Mazur was baffled but, as he recalls, ". . . didn't get the message– quite yet." On subsequent examinations he paired simple qualitative questions with more difficult quantitative problems on the same physical concepts. While about half of his students did equally well (or poorly) on both quantitative and qualitative questions, 40 percent did better calculating answers to formulas than resolving the conceptual issues on which the problems were based. Slowly, the pieces of the puzzle fell into place.

> Students concentrate on learning "recipes," or "problem-solving strategies". . . without bothering to be attentive to the underlying concepts. This explained the blunders I had seen from apparently bright students. Problem-solving strategies work on some but not all problems. No wonder students were frustrated with physics. How boring physics must be when it is reduced to a set of mechanical recipes without any apparent logic. Newton's third law is *obviously* right, but how do I convince my students? Certainly not by just reciting the law and then blindly using it in problems.[3]

Converted to a new cause, Mazur embarked on what he now calls his "little crusade." Hestenes' paper had alerted him to what was wrong, but there was no clear prescription as to what to do about it. How do you deal with persistent misconceptions, particularly in the large lecture class which is so typical of introductory physics?[4] Aware that at most large universities any useful innovation would have to be compatible with large classes and not demand additional time from an instructor or TA (that is, additional funds), Mazur realized he would have to make small changes that would, in total, have a large and lasting impact. Teaching physics to small groups of students–Mazur's first idea–would simply not be possible at most places.[5]

---

[2] Eric Mazur, "Qualitative vs. Quantitative Thinking: Are We Teaching the Right Thing?" *Optics & Photonics News*, February 1992, p. 38.

[3] Ibid.

[4] While Hestenes is reluctant to tell instructors specifically what to do, his group is now offering summer institutes in "modeling instruction in mechanics" for high school teachers. See David Hestenes, Malcolm Wells, and Greg Swackhamer, "Force Concept Inventory," *The Physics Teacher, 30*, March 1992, pp. 141-151, and the announcement of a summer program, p. 151.

[5] At Rutgers, where Mazur has recently given a talk about peer instruction in the large

He began by interviewing half of the 200 students he was then teaching. In twenty minutes with each he confirmed the truth of research on misconceptions in introductory physics. They were rife among students. Meanwhile, he made an interesting observation: when he started a discussion in lab with one student, other students would take the dialogue further. Students have many advantages over their instructor in explaining difficult ideas to one another, Mazur noticed. Things that are obvious to a trained physicist are not yet obvious to them. Ignorant of the subject's jargon, they find other ways to convey what they are trying to understand. "They know where the difficulty lies, how to simplify an issue and, in language their peers can understand, how to express it." Students, he concluded, could be patient, empathic and, if there were no grading on a curve,[6] enthusiastic about peer instruction. Mazur decided to try to integrate discussion cycles into his lecture class.

There was support for this reform, because coverage in introductory physics had long been a topic of discussion within Mazur's department. During the summer of 1990 he compared old textbooks with current editions, noting that the older the text, the more detailed the conceptual explanation of each topic. Textbooks had become so overburdened with derivations, examples, and problems that there was no need to regurgitate them to the class. If he could get his students to read the text in advance and provide them with his ideas as printed notes, he might be able to save most of the time spent on problem solving. In the time thus freed up he could engage his students in what he calls peer instruction cycles.

Beginning in the fall of 1991, he says, "I just did it." In addition to detailed lecture notes (printed and available from his office), Mazur found or created five new "thought" questions for each ninety-minute class. He begins by sharing his goals with his students. He wants them to learn to "critically reason" about physics, not merely memorize equations. To accomplish this he insists that they prepare by reading the text in advance of each lecture. To motivate them to stay on schedule he gives a five-minute, graded, one-question quiz every class on the conceptual content of the reading assignment, a question not difficult to answer if the material has been read. Thereafter, the class is divided into segments as follows.

---

lecture course in physics, there are 700 students taking introductory physics in each entering class.

[6] Mazur had never employed curved grading. On the contrary, his course handout had always made it perfectly clear that a certain number of points in the course would translate into a certain letter grade; even students who had not done well early on in the course had the possibility of an "A" if they did well on the final.

A ten- or fifteen-minute lecture is followed immediately by a display on the viewgraph of a "simple" conceptual multiple choice question (the "Conceptest") to which students record after a minute or so both an answer and a confidence level ("pretty sure," "not quite sure," "just guessing"). Then they discuss the question and their answer with a neighbor. Mazur's directions: "Try to convince your neighbor of your answer."[7] The single voice in an otherwise silent classroom is instantly transformed into a buzz of earnest discussion. Mazur watches and waits. After another minute his students record a second, possibly revised answer (and revised confidence level) on the same machine-readable sheet.[8] Then there is a straw poll. If most have gotten the answer right, he moves on. If 40 percent or more got it wrong, he repeats the cycle on the same topic. "The system," he says, "prevents any great gulf from developing between my expectations and those of the class." He knows immediately what his students have grasped and what they need more help on.

Teaching this way requires preparation, but not the volumes of lecture notes Mazur has assembled over many years of introductory physics. For this revised format it is more important to prepare the quick quiz he gives at the beginning, and the five concept questions asked during lecture. Not knowing which questions students will find difficult, Mazur cannot predict which topics will require additional explanation, so he has to be able to improvise. But it is worth the effort. Just as Mazur has to be very alert, no student can sleep or daydream through class. "I put them on the spot at least five times during the class hour, but because their answers are recorded only to give me feedback, they're not under pressure."

Eliminating derivations, problems, and examples from lecture has not affected learning. Mazur explains to students that he doesn't deal with these in class, not because they are unimportant, but because they're in the book.[9] "There's no point wasting their time and mine going over these in class." There was a time in his former life, he says, when the brightest students would ask him for more and more difficult practice problems, as exams consisted only of problems. Today's exams include concepts and qualitative essay questions of his devising. "But if class discussion calls for a difficult problem," Mazur adds, "I can always find one in my old notes."

---

[7] The technique is not unlike the "Whimbey Pairs" employed at University of Wisconsin-Eau Claire (see chap. 2, p. 29). There, however, talking-to-your-neighbor was employed on an as-needed basis. Mazur structures his lecture around five scheduled cycles of peer instruction.

[8] The sheets are handed in at the end of the class for purposes of data collection, not to be graded.

[9] Problem solving is handled in recitation sections run by teaching assistants.

Paul Martin, dean of the division of applied sciences at Harvard, encouraged Mazur with a small grant to cover the salaries of a postdoc and two extra TAs. The extra help has made the search for good questions easier. (Mazur insists there are many publications from which faculty could cull such questions, but he plans to publish his in the near future.) A modest one-year Pew Charitable Trust grant of $50,000 has helped document students' performance which, in turn, will allow Mazur to quantify the results of his technique with hard and–he hopes–*convincing* data so the technique can be systematized and widely applied. He is convinced that his students are doing better, not just on the Mechanics Baseline Examination (now called the Force Concept Inventory) which he continues to give them, but on more traditional problem-solving tests as well.[10] Most of all, he believes that lectures mixed with peer instruction address the "primary factors contributing to students' frustration and consequent difficulties with introductory college science and engineering courses."[11]

Mazur is a pragmatist. He was looking for a simple and convenient way of eliciting and monitoring students' understanding. And he thinks he found it. The technique requires no capital investment and little preparation other than a suitable set of conceptual questions. The rewards, however, are substantial for students and instructor alike. He writes:

> When the students are asked to convince their neighbors of the validity of each other's choices, *all* students are suddenly involved in the lecture. Because there is no faculty-student pressure, the discussion is completely uninhibited–for the faculty member, the experience of standing in front of [an animated] class of students is exhilarating.[12]

In addition to breaking the monotony of passive lectures, the remarkable improvements in the percentage of correct answers in class and on both standard and Hestenes-Halloun type examinations demonstrates to

---

[10] Average posttest scores on the Hestenes-Halloun Force Concept Inventory and Baseline tests for Mazur's 1991 class (223 students) are 85 percent and 72 percent respectively, a clear improvement over the 1990 scores of 77 percent and 66 percent. The pretest-posttest gain was 17 percent for the 1991 class compared with a modest 9 percent gain for the 1990 class. Even more interesting, most of the gain was at the lower end of the distribution. As reported in David Hestenes and Malcolm Wells, "A Mechanics Baseline Test," *The Physics Teacher, 30,* March 1992, p. 162.

[11] Eric Mazur, "Stimulating Renewed Interest in Science, Mathematics and Engineering by Peer Instruction," a proposal to the NSF Undergraduate Course and Curriculum Development Program, September 16, 1991, p. 6.

[12] Ibid.

Mazur the effectiveness of the method. Even after just a minute or so of discussion, "the force of clear thinking usually overwhelms common sense misconceptions." Not only is the technique doable in a large class, but Mazur believes it works better because there is a reasonable number of students who *do* understand the concept, enough to make "peer instruction" work.

Other benefits, reports David Hall, a graduate student in physics and a TA for the course, are a cooperative rather than competitive class environment; a chance to verbalize physical concepts; and, due to the qualitative nature of the questions, a de-emphasis on calculations. Furthermore, should students become lost during lecture, discussion during Conceptests gives them time to catch up and helps them pinpoint weak spots in their conceptual understanding of the material. Altogether the course makes students aware of the need to correctly interpret physical phenomena.

One of the several reasons Mazur has enjoyed support for his effort to improve his lecture course is Harvard's Bok Center for Teaching and Learning which encourages collaborative and interactive learning. In a Bok Center video released in 1991 two other faculty join Mazur in a display of variants of peer instruction.[13] Chemistry professor James Davis trains his TAs to encourage group problem solving in the recitation sections of a large introductory chemistry course, and astronomer Philip Sadler teaches entirely by group work. Students interviewed for the video talk about "being involved," about "having to think *while* we're learning," and about having to come to class better prepared. Perhaps the most convincing statement is that of a student in Mazur's class who understands that "if I can figure something out for myself, I will probably be able to figure it out on the exam, and [best of all] for the rest of my life."

Of course there is no guarantee that students will take the time to really absorb and retain conceptual underpinnings of problems. Hall reports that when Mazur momentarily forgets to give the right answer after discussing a particular conceptual question or Conceptest, the students are impatient to know what it is. Does this mean they aren't following the reasoning, Hall asks, or are they so insecure that they want the professor's response as reinforcement? Another concern is retention. Hall notes that when a Conceptest is given out of context, students sometimes don't do as well. Newton's third law, for example, heavily emphasized in physics 11A, was sometimes forgotten when the application was to electrostatic, rather than mechanical, forces as in physics 11B. Still, the discussion of

---

[13] "Thinking Together: Collaborative Learning in Science," The Derek Bok Teaching and Learning Center, Harvard University.

concepts has an important role. Hall writes:

> Lectures without Conceptests [now] seem long to me, and I
> can imagine that the students find them less engaging, too.
> When one is used to Conceptests, it can be difficult to live
> without them.

Like Layzer and Herschbach's chem-phys,[14] physics 11 is not a course
for the physics major. Mazur thinks it is the place where "second tier"
students might be recruited to science and that, if large numbers of
students experience physics more positively, the public's perception of
science will be improved. Hall doubts that the technique would be as well
received by physics majors as by those with only a passing commitment
to the discipline, and feels that the Conceptest and peer discussion might
be considered condescending. The real test of Mazur's technique, then,
will come when instructors at other levels of physics decide to substitute
discussion and debate for full-time lecturing.

In 1991, in order to convince his critics, Mazur agreed (with some
trepidation) to expose physics 11 students to one of his old (and very
tough) problem-solving examinations. When his students on average
scored seven to ten points higher (out of 100) than their predecessors who
had taken a more traditional lecture course in 1985, his point was made.
Now plans are in the works to try out variants of the peer instruction
method in Harvard's algebra-based physics course, physics 1, and in the
faster-moving physics 15.

Propagation

Other variants of peer instruction in physics are being implemented at
a variety of institutions. Ever since Mazur described the idea at a meeting
of the American Association of Physics Teachers he has been inundated
with requests for details from diverse institutions. At Appalachian State
University (ASU), as one example of how rapidly peer instruction can be
modified and applied elsewhere, physicist Patricia Allen returned from
the AAPT meeting and contacted her coinstructor[15] to propose a modification of Mazur's technique in the very next (second) semester of
calculus-based physics. Instead of four Conceptests and discussions per
lecture period, Allen and Walter Connelly introduce about two a week.
Like Mazur, the two North Carolina physicists are collecting first and
second answers (and confidence levels) on Conceptests for analysis.

---

[14] See chapter 6.

[15] The course at Appalachian State University is taught in two independent sections of
approximately fifty students each.

They are looking forward to comparing the results of 1992's final exam with 1991 as a measure of the effectiveness of peer instruction.

So far, Allen is intrigued by gender differences in stated confidence levels in answering Conceptest questions. Males start out far more confident (even about what they don't know), lose confidence in the middle, and then slowly regain it. Females are lower in confidence at the beginning and grow steadily more confident as the semester progresses. And there are other interesting changes, she says:

> The class is active, not just during the discussion of the Conceptest, but afterwards. They are asking more questions and not just the "how do I solve . . ." kind. They talk more outside of class, and seem to have formed ongoing study groups.[16]

What she likes best, as does Mazur, is that by testing students on material they may not know, she can uncover gaps early on. She adjusts her coverage immediately, no longer having to wait for an in-class examination to tell her what she needs to cover in greater depth or detail.

The students in calculus-based physics at Appalachian State are not necessarily matriculating in either physics or engineering. They are first-generation college goers, and one-third to one-half are majoring in education (mostly math education). This may eventually facilitate the introduction of the instruction method into the high school, Allen says.

Student Response

How are students responding to the new lecture format? Mazur wants to believe that it provides enough structure to prevent floundering, but at the same time is open enough to engage students' curiosities. To get students' views of the project TA Wayne Yang interviewed two biology concentrators taking physics 11 to fulfill a requirement, and a literature concentrator who selected physics 11 both to deepen his understanding of chemistry and out of sheer curiosity about physics.

The lecture format, Conceptests, and the ensuing discussion get high marks from these very different students. But when questions about concepts appear on final examinations, attitudes are more mixed. One student liked being able to justify her answer in essay form, while another felt the conceptual questions were too tricky. The literature major was originally attracted to physics 11 for its grading on an absolute scale and not on a curve. "It looked like it was going to be friendly," he reported. At the end he found the course tough, well-taught, and time-consuming.

---

[16] Personal communication to the author.

Overall, Yang reports students equally praise Mazur's ability to teach physics and his commitment and concern with their learning. He is often applauded at the end of the ninety-minute lectures, and 90 percent of those enrolled regularly attend. Students quite obviously enjoy his classes.

Conclusion

What's interesting about Mazur's modification of introductory physics is that it is a *modification*, not a radical departure. In describing the course David Hall notes that the lectures are very similar *in content* to those he took as an undergraduate. The material is presented in the same order as the textbook, although Mazur sometimes goes into more detail about a particular subject. One difference previously noted is that the emphasis is on exposition rather than problem solving. Mazur will talk about the history of physical laws, for example, especially in the electricity and magnetism semester. Accompanying the exposition are demonstrations, usually spectacular, Hall reports, owing to Harvard's full-time demonstration staff. But it is the Conceptest which makes the class unique. "If you take away the Conceptests," Hall says, "little would distinguish physics 11 from other introductory courses."

In theory, this means that after watching a video on how Mazur organizes his course, instructors elsewhere could do it themselves. Once Mazur publishes a full set of Conceptests for the two-semester calculus-based physics course, presumably, he could retire as an innovator. But in fact the ease with which peer instruction can be added to the mainstream physics course is deceptive. It's like the old light bulb joke, as told by psychologists. What is going to make the physics community (the light bulb in this case) really *want* to change?[17]

---

[17] "How many economists (physicists, bureaucrats, etc.) does it take to change a light bulb?" The psychologists' answer: "Just one, but the light bulb has to *want* to change."

Affirmative Education
California State University, Los Angeles

On April 15, 1991, *Chemical & Engineering News*, read regularly by 350,000 chemists in academe and industry, published a special report on minorities in science.[1] The collective impact of efforts to increase participation of historically underrepresented minorities in science, the report concluded, "has been disappointing."[2] Membership in the American Chemical Society (ACS), for example, remained 98 percent white and Asian in 1990, just as it had been in 1975. Of the 1,286 Ph.D. degrees awarded in chemistry to U.S. citizens in 1989, only sixty-five, or 5 percent, went to underrepresented minorities. What was learned over the past two decades was "what doesn't work," Luther Williams of NSF's Directorate for Education and Human Resources was quoted as saying.

Much of the focus (of the article and of funded projects) was on a precollege educational system that doesn't serve minorities well, this according to authorities like George Castro, president of the Society for Advancement of Chicanos and Native Americans in Science (SACNAS). Public schools with the highest minority enrollments also have the lowest average family income and are much more likely to be in inner cities. They have fewer resources and offer fewer math and science courses than do schools with predominantly white students.[3] The prevailing belief seems to be that expressed by Joseph Danek of NSF's human resources development division: "By the time [students] are seventeen years old, they are either in or out; if they don't perform within those years . . . everything closes down for them."[4]

---

[1] "Minorities in Science," *Chemical & Engineering News*, Vol. 69, No. 15, April 15, 1991, pp. 20-35.

[2] Ibid., p. 21.

[3] Ibid., p. 24, quoting a 1989 Rand Corporation study undertaken by Jeannie Oakes, now professor of education at UCLA.

[4] Ibid., p. 25.

Because of that view, programs for K-12 minorities are better funded than programs for minority undergraduates. Only in the past two years has NSF created the Alliances for Minority Participation program, which offers five-year grants at $1 million per year to coalitions of undergraduate institutions in regions that serve minority students. But one model stands out among programs that work for minority undergraduates: the Minority Biomedical Research Support program (MBRS). Funded by the National Institutes of Health (NIH), MBRS was established in 1972 to address the shortage of minority students in the biomedical sciences, and focused on institutions that graduated the largest numbers of minorities. The program's first thirty-eight schools were mostly black colleges and universities, but it later expanded to include southwestern schools with predominantly Hispanic enrollments, and a growing number of large, inner-city universities with sizable enrollments of both black and Hispanic students.

Beginning with $2 million in 1972, MBRS is now budgeted at $42 million and operates at about 100 schools. Some 500 MBRS students get bachelor's degrees every year, and 80 percent of them go on to some form of postgraduate study, half in the health professions and half in Ph.D. programs.[5] This outstanding record belies the fact that MBRS targets academically average minority students with GPAs as low as 2.0. How does MBRS accomplish its aims? What kind of environment must be in place to sustain this successful exercise in "affirmative education?" The Department of Chemistry-Biochemistry at California State University, Los Angeles (henceforth Cal State LA), site of one of the longest continuing MBRS programs in the nation, provides some clues.

The Demographics

Of the 361,000 students enrolled in the twenty campuses of the California State University System in 1988-89, only 101 black, American Indian, and Hispanic students were expected to graduate with majors in physical science or mathematics.[6] These figures are disputed, but even if minority physical science and mathematics majors are underestimated by several hundreds, their low percentage underscores the need to attract and retain minority students in science. Cal State LA is located in northeastern Los Angeles, in an urban center distinguished by an un-

---

[5] Ibid., p. 30, quoting Ciriaco Q. Gonzales, director of MBRS at NIH.

[6] These numbers taken from the "Report: 1988-89 CSU Bachelor's Degrees Awarded to Underrepresented Minorities in Engineering and Science." Source the CSU Chancellor's Office, Long Beach, Calif.

usual degree of racial and cultural diversity in its population. Within a fifteen-mile radius of the school lie the black community of Watts, a barrio of Mexican-Americans, Chinatown, Little Tokyo, and Koreatown. The surrounding communities, which have experienced increasing Asian and Hispanic in-migration in recent decades, also feed the school. Since the college recruits largely from its immediate neighborhood, it is not surprising that the fall quarter 1990 figures show that only 27.5 percent of the 21,596 students enrolled are classified as "white, non-Hispanics," and of the 72.5 percent minority students, 32.2 percent are Hispanic, 28.4 percent Asian-Pacific islanders, 11.4 percent black, and .5 percent native American. The average age of all students is 25, and 57.5 percent are female. Only 72.2 percent are U.S. citizens; the remainder are classified as "visa students," "immigrants," or "refugees."

For those of us who concentrated full time on our studies in college, it is difficult to imagine the complexity of some of these students' lives. Many are married and have families requiring financial support and time away from academic pursuits. Recent immigrants find parents and relatives sometimes returning to the countries from which they emigrated, leaving their more Americanized offspring to fend for themselves. For students like these, majoring in science at college is probably the most challenging course of study they could pursue. The demanding curriculum, coupled with laboratories requiring many additional hours, contribute to their real personal difficulties in completing these majors.

Still, science is appealing. The material is culture-blind, and the knowledge and skills acquired seem certain of recognition and remuneration. There is the possibility of a career in medicine, with its disproportionate rewards. And there is a traditional pathway, so far little traveled by postwar minority populations, to upward mobility through science and engineering. So it is not surprising that many new minority students want to major in science or engineering. But it takes part-time science majors seven or more years to graduate. And 30 to 55 percent fail or change to nonscience fields during their first two years of college.[7]

The State University System

The California master plan for higher education designates three separate higher education systems: the University of California (UC), the

[7] The Minority Science Program Report, prepared by Margaret Jefferson of biology and Raymond Garcia of chemistry-biochemistry, scans ten science departments at Cal State LA. It shows a disproportionately high number of Asians (45.6 percent), and fewer Hispanics, blacks, whites, and females majoring in science, compared to the general population at the college (April 1990, p. 3).

California State University (CSU), and the two-year community colleges. Each has different functions, responsibilities, and entrance requirements. Whereas the UC campuses accept the top 12.5 percent of graduating high school seniors, the CSU campuses accept the top 30 percent, a population with poorer academic records and lower SAT scores. CSU gives these students access to an undergraduate education, some masters' programs and, in some selected cases, a Ph.D. degree in conjunction with one of the state's public or private universities.

Within this framework, Cal State LA can be described as an undergraduate liberal arts and science campus with some ancillary professional programs in business and in nursing. It offers bachelor's and master's degrees in most disciplines, and a Ph.D. degree jointly with UCLA in special education.[8] The Department of Chemistry-Biochemistry offers B.S. degrees in both disciplines with honors options, a B.A. degree in chemistry (with less stringent requirements), and an M.S. with an option in biochemistry. The department's program is approved by the ACS.

The successful recruitment and retention of minorities in science at Cal State LA results from several factors. One is that several departments have managed to attract research-minded Ph.D.s who come to Cal State LA to continue their research along with teaching. Since most of the available research assistants are undergraduates, the faculty set out to design and develop an undergraduate research component for its majors long before outside funding for minorities became available.

At any one time there are more than fifty undergraduates doing research with the faculty in chemistry-biochemistry. Of these some will get course credit for directed study, others will take units of honors studies in chemistry, and many will complete a research project and write and defend a thesis embodying their research. Cal State LA thus joins a number of institutions, elite private as well as state-funded schools, where the faculty *insists* that research experience, especially in chemistry, is more valuable to a student than additional coursework. Undergraduates are better served, it is maintained, by a faculty that pursues research than one involved solely in teaching. What makes Cal State LA's program noteworthy is that minority students are targeted in their sophomore year (most begin a research project in their junior year), and there is real evidence that this is what gets them hooked on science.

Associated with a young and growing institution, the chemistry-biochemistry department has shaped itself around both teaching and research. Recruiting in the early postwar years, recalls Tony Andreoli,

---

[8] In the entire CSU system there is only one joint Ph.D. in chemistry, offered by San Diego State University in conjunction with UC, San Diego.

professor of biochemistry and the department's senior member, he enlisted the services of young research-oriented Ph.D.s who wanted to teach in an urban school and continue their research. In the growth years of the 1960s and 1970s senior faculty consciously recruited additional members who shared the department's philosophy and goals. An external reviewer, evaluating the department a few years ago, commented that "The core of the senior faculty . . . must be given the credit for the wisdom and foresight to understand the unique opportunity offered here. They were dedicated to the education of undergraduates, to the incorporation of minority undergraduates in the programs, to an active research program, and to recruitment of new faculty dedicated to the philosophy of utilizing undergraduates as the major research tool."[9] Indeed, long before the MBRS program was initiated, the stage was set for chemistry-biochemistry at Cal State LA to take advantage of minority undergraduate research support.

Funding

When the definition of "minority institution" was expanded from its original focus on historically black institutions, Cal State LA, with its overwhelming minority population and its preexisting undergraduate research programs, readily qualified. Within a year of the MBRS program's creation, Cal State LA received one of the grants in 1972. Under the leadership of Lloyd Ferguson until 1984, this interdepartmental program, with chemistry-biochemistry and biology the main players, began an eighteen-year relationship that has generated nearly $17 million in grants.[10] In 1984, Tony Andreoli became the director of the program and under his leadership the funding has increased to $1.3 million in 1990, allocated in four-year funding cycles, distributed to qualifying principal investigators for research involving minority undergraduates and graduate students.[11]

This long-term, continuous support allowed Cal State LA to develop an infrastructure which sponsors research of such a caliber that the faculty has become competitive in seeking grants under other programs and from other sources. Supplemental grants from MBRS for instrumentation, coupled with matching university funds, made possible the

---

[9] External review of the programs of the Department of Chemistry-Biochemistry, 1986.

[10] The program also includes the Departments of Biology, Microbiology, Psychology and Family Studies and Consumer Affairs.

[11] Lloyd Ferguson was the first director of the MBRS program at Cal State LA starting out in 1973 with a budget of $228,678 per year and remaining in that position until 1984.

acquisition of first-class equipment, including costly NMR and electron spin resonance spectrometers, mass spectrometers and the like–supplies essential for state-of-the-art chemical and biochemical research.

Graduates of the Department

During the past twenty years, chemistry-biochemistry at Cal State LA has graduated an average of fifteen majors a year, twenty-five in some peak years in the late 1970s. Neither the rate nor the accrual (400 in the past twenty years) is modest, and the numbers compare favorably to much larger and better endowed universities where, of the hundreds, sometimes thousands, of students enrolled in introductory chemistry, only one in fifty may complete the major. Detailed records of ethnicity and postgraduate work have been kept for only ten years, but fully half of the 182 graduates in chemistry-biochemistry between 1980 and 1989 (counting Asian-Americans) were minority.

Most of these students have not stopped at the B.S. level. Of the 182 graduates between 1980 and 1989 sixty-six attended graduate schools, some at UC campuses (Irvine, Berkeley, Davis, Riverside, Los Angeles), some at private Eastern institutions such as Cornell, Yale, Purdue, and Johns Hopkins, and an additional twenty-eight chose professional schools. Most importantly, 90 percent of the students who entered Ph.D. programs completed the degree, an outstanding proportion when one examines national statistics.[12]

Undergraduate Research

Most of the sixty to eighty undergraduate students served by these research programs in the chemistry-biochemistry department would not have been able to "do science"–they are quick to tell the visitor–without the combination of financial support, encouragement, and pure dedication of the faculty. The department is a beehive of activity, with a typical research group including juniors and seniors, an occasional sophomore, and a few master's candidates mixed in. Some students are funded by MBRS, some by MARC (NIH's Minority Access to Research Careers program, see page 137), and others are simply honors students or in the undergraduate directed-study course. Since the department also attracts research grants based solely on scientific merit, still more undergradu-

---

[12]Harold Goldwhite and Tom Onak, "Undergraduate Research in Chemistry at California State University, Los Angeles," *CUR* (Council on Undergraduate Research) *Newsletter,* Vol. 8, 1988, p. 25.

ates can be paid to assist.[13] Immediately obvious to the outsider touring the lab is the range of ethnicity and academic competence; noteworthy are the students' intensity, willingness to help each other, and high morale.

Faculty researchers have developed plans of action for dealing with students who may not be performing well academically, and who may not have decided on science as a career. It can be time-consuming, for these are novice students who had no encouragement to "play" at science at home. They need to build self-confidence, to discipline themselves, and to find rewards in their studies and in research participation.

Recognizing the demands of supervising MBRS research, the NIH grants 20 percent release time to a principal investigator and two-thirds summer salary when student laboratory work is at a peak. Faculty members who supervise MARC students receive 7 percent release time. Another endorsement of the department's commitment to minority students comes from the university, which provides matching funds for major equipment purchases.

Faculty Commitment

Much of the success of Cal State LA's minority science program is due to the dedication and diversity of its faculty. Of the seventeen members in the department, six can be classified as members of ethnic minorities.[14] There have been one or more black faculty members in chemistry-biochemistry since 1968.

Since chemistry-biochemistry became a separate department in 1959 it has grown from three to seventeen full-time faculty. All hold Ph.D. degrees and most had postdoctoral or industrial experience before coming to Cal State LA. Their teaching skills have been recognized by a disproportionately large number of "outstanding professor awards" (twelve), and system-wide "trustee awards" (five). With the selection of Phoebe Dea as the system-wide outstanding professor in 1991, five of Cal State LA's ten teaching awards had been won by chemistry-biochemistry. Cal State LA's president James Rosser calls the department " . . . one of the leading undergraduate science [teaching] departments in the nation."[15]

---

[13] From, for example, the ACS's Petroleum Research Fund (ACS-PRF), Research Corporation, Department of Energy, etc.

[14] The department currently has one black member, two Mexican-Americans, one Latino, and two women, of whom one, Phoebe Dea, is a Chinese-American.

[15] According to another external reviewer, "The department excels by all standards: teaching awards, publications, research funds awarded, funding opportunities for pro-

Contrary to conventional wisdom, teaching does not compete with, but complements research in the department. Teacher-student interactions in the context of the research program *contribute* to high research productivity rather than *detract* from it. When it comes to promotions, excellence in teaching is measured not just in student course evaluations, but in the number of students in the faculty member's research group and that member's initiative in organizing new courses and seminars. Promotions are also based on professional growth as measured by number of grants and number of publications (including those done with students). A last category, here as elsewhere, is called *service* and refers to committee membership and service to the department and the university.

Evidence that excellence in teaching need not conflict with research productivity is revealed by grants and publications. Fifteen faculty members have external support for at least part of their research activity—a high proportion for an undergraduate institution. The average annual total of such grants for the years 1986-1990 was $1.4 million. In number of publications since 1967, chemistry-biochemistry was the most productive department of the twenty CSU campuses. From 1962 to 1990 there were 394 publications and meeting presentations, many of them coauthored with undergraduates, published in refereed journals, and presented at scientific meetings. The average publication rate over a decade was ten-fifteen journal articles and four books and/or reviews per year.

The release time given faculty in minority research programs contributes to productivity and to faculty enthusiasm for them. The units release time per term produces 20 percent more time for contacts with individual students and for research.

Tom Onak, recipient of the 1990 ACS Award for Research in Undergraduate Education, has been at Cal State LA since 1959, during which time he has written 115 papers on carborane chemistry with forty student coauthors. Of the total sixty-one students who have worked in Onak's lab, ten have been female and thirty-four have been minorities: Hispanic (seven), black (six), Asian (twenty-one). Eleven of these students have completed either Ph.D.s or M.D.s, and six are currently working toward graduate degrees.

Lloyd Ferguson, who in 1943 became the first black to receive a Ph.D. in chemistry from UC-Berkeley, was a well-established educator when he came to Cal State LA in 1965. He had been chairman of chemistry at Howard University when the department established its Ph.D. program, one that subsequently trained 60 to 70 percent of all the black Ph.D.

---

fessional enhancement, helping minority students and others to develop professional careers, involvement in local and national professional societies, and it has played a significant role in the administrative functions of the university."

chemists currently working. He garnered many national awards for his outstanding contribution to chemical education and his leadership in the black scientific community. Ferguson, who is now emeritus, has in the past decade guided twenty-five minority students through his lab.

The principle that the chemistry-biochemistry faculty should reflect the ethnic diversity of the student body directs recruitment. As chairman of the department in 1976, Tony Fratiello actively supported the hiring of Phoebe Dea, a female Asian, and Carlos Gutierrez, a Mexican-American. Sixteen years later both Gutierrez and Dea are in leadership roles, Gutierrez as department chairman, a director of the MARC program, and, as of 1992, MBRS director as well; Phoebe Dea as a distinguished teacher and one of the department's leading grants recipients. Cal State LA's minority faculty act as role models for minority students. So it is no surprise that Phoebe Dea's lab has a preponderance of Asian-American females, or that Ray Garcia's lab attracts Hispanics.

Among these minority faculty, Anthony J. Andreoli epitomizes his own and the department's conviction that scholarship, teaching, and mentoring of minority students naturally combine. There is no way, everyone tells me, that the minority programs at Cal State LA would have been so successful had it not been for Tony Andreoli. Born of Costa Rican immigrant parents, Andreoli earned a bachelor's degree on the G.I. Bill and a Ph.D. in 1955. He came to the then-new Los Angeles State College of Applied Arts and Sciences (now Cal State LA) in 1955 and, though technically emeritus, still manages the minority support programs he helped design. Throughout a long career, which in 1956 included receiving the first NSF grant ever awarded to Cal State LA and serving as MBRS program director for the past decade, Andreoli has demonstrated that teaching, scholarship, and research are inseparable. As the winner of the AAAS's Mentor Award for 1991, Andreoli was cited "for his efforts to encourage and guide generations of minority students to pursue postdoctoral study of the sciences."

Tony Fratiello, a physical chemist at Cal State LA since 1963, grew up in a middle-class Italian-American family in Providence, Rhode Island. After attending a parochial high school and college, Fratiello moved to the more diverse atmosphere of Brown University for his Ph.D. An active researcher, studying the multinuclear magnetic resonance of metal ion solution-complexes, he has ushered some sixty students through their studies and published an equal number of papers (fifty with undergraduate coauthors). He has served as department chairman and was director of the Research Improvement for Minority Institutions program (RIMI) from 1986-1990, a $100,000-per-year initiative sponsoring ten minority students per quarter.

Costello Brown attended segregated black schools in rural North Carolina through college. Sheltered from racial tensions in his childhood, he first encountered racism when he left the South to earn a Ph.D. at Iowa State in Ames in the early 1960s. This exposure, coupled with his participation as a student in sit-ins in the South, honed his sensitivity to minority issues and shaped his goals. He received his Ph.D. in 1968 and was recruited in 1969 by Lloyd Ferguson, already a role model for young black chemists. Like his colleagues in the department, he is most proud of those minority students suffering from low self-esteem and bound for uncertain academic careers at larger, impersonal institutions, who have turned their lives around at Cal State LA.

Another faculty mentor eager to help minority students carve careers in science is Ray Garcia. A professor of biochemistry since 1982, Garcia is of well-educated Mexican-American parentage. His family, which now includes numerous physicians, Ph.D.s, and pharmacists, came to Texas at the turn of the century driving 5,000 head of cattle, and quickly established itself in the community. Eager to help students advance and move out from the Los Angeles barrio, Garcia participates enthusiastically as a faculty adviser in the university-wide Minority Science Program. He speaks with great passion about the forty or so students who have come through his lab. Eighteen were in the minority undergraduate programs, mostly Mexican-Americans. Six of his undergraduate lab assistants have received B.S. degrees, two M.A.s, one a D.O., one an M.D., one a D.D.S.; five are in medical school and two are in Ph.D. programs.

A different picture emerges from the other two members of the department. Phoebe Dea was born in Canton, China and grew up in Hong Kong, leaving her family behind to go to UCLA. Not particularly affected by discrimination against females or Asians, she graduated in 1967 and completed a Ph.D. in chemistry at Caltech in 1972. Since joining Cal State's faculty in 1976, Phoebe Dea has devoted much attention to research with undergraduates. Many students now in graduate school voice the same sentiments as a recent graduate winner of the science and scholarship award of the Westinghouse Talent Search—namely, that Phoebe Dea was the "one person most influential in my career development." In addition to receiving the 1991 California State University Outstanding Professor Award, she was chosen as the 1991 California Professor of the Year by the Council for the Advancement and Support of Education, a national organization.

It doesn't take long for Phoebe Dea to describe how she brings MBRS students up to speed in her research lab. Her goal is to "develop scientific expertise," but she also wants to cultivate students' self-confidence and give them some sense of the excitement of doing research. To build impetus she works side by side with MBRS students until they get their first experimental results. She starts with a simple project to give the student a sense of the time and effort it takes to plan and carry out a successful new experiment. Only when the data is in hand is the student sent out to read related papers to see where his or her work fits in. "When the students realize that they have gotten a result 'like a scientist,' their fears and doubts disappear," says Dea.

A similar role is played by department chairman Carlos Gutierrez, director of MARC since 1983. His Ph.D. from UC-Davis in 1975 led initially to a one-year, and then to a permanent, appointment at Cal State LA in organic chemistry. In those fifteen years Gutierrez has become a leader in minority science education. His research projects involve a range of general synthetic techniques, particularly chelating agents, natural products chemistry, and organo-tin compounds. His research assistants include an Asian, an Armenian, an Argentinian, a Canadian, two Chicanos, and one black–all undergraduates, and five of the eleven are women.

The MBRS Program at Cal State LA

Individual attention, research opportunities, mentoring, and incremental success are needed for minority students to succeed in science, but they are insufficient if students have to hold a job outside of school twenty to forty additional hours per week. MBRS provides minority undergraduates a salary of $6,000 for fifteen hours a week of laboratory work during the school year, and full-time work in the summer. The salary for master's candidates is $7,500. The money and the "work-for-salary ethic" of the MBRS are much appreciated by minority students. "It is more of a real-life situation than an academic one," says an MBRS undergraduate.

In addition to student salaries and faculty release time MBRS provides funds for travel to scientific meetings where participants present their work. As students strongly indicated, this travel is highly valued, not just for the experience (although for some these were their first trips out of the barrio), but for the sense of being accepted in "the alien world of science and scientists." After these exposures students begin to believe what their mentors have been telling them: that they can fit in, and that a career in science is a reasonable goal.

The benefits of MBRS to students are obvious, but so are the benefits to faculty–benefits, they say, which more than compensate for the time taken to train initially low-achieving students to do research. Every faculty member who participates in MBRS writes a section of an NIH proposal as part of a single omnibus application for every four-year cycle. Costello Brown, who has served on a number of NIH and NSF review panels, says that evaluation of the proposal is based on the scientific merit of the project, its biomedical relevancy, and the students' potential benefit. Since teaching loads are heavy at Cal State LA (twelve units of teaching and three units of advising per quarter for three quarters), the 20 percent release time for participating faculty is welcome, and provides time to supervise students doing research. Faculty claim that the undergraduates' research contribution is almost equivalent to what one would expect of graduate RAs. The undergraduates work as well, but "more slowly." Indeed, the eighteen MBRS faculty in the five departments typically produce twenty-five to twenty-eight papers per year, coauthored with their minority students.

The most valuable MBRS benefits are those to students: over the past eighteen years 603 minority students have been employed in five participating departments, with chemistry-biochemistry and biology taking in the majority. To date the 603 received 265 B.S. degrees, ninety-five B.A.s, and fifty M.S.s, a success rate of 70 percent. Of those who completed postgraduate work at other institutions, sixteen have received Ph.D.s, nineteen D.D.S. degrees, fifty-seven M.D.s, one a D.V.M., two degrees in pharmacy, and four degrees in osteopathy. Still in progress are twenty-one in Ph.D. programs, sixty-four in medicine, twenty-two master's candidates, fourteen D.D.S., and eleven in health-related disciplines. That represents 50 percent of the students entering the program, some with GPAs as low as 2.00. Lloyd Ferguson, the previous director, calls this a "fantastic success rate." About 95 percent of those who apply to graduate or professional schools are admitted, a percentage, Ferguson estimates, about five times what it would be in the absence of the MBRS program.

This is a potent argument, says Andreoli, for not restricting research opportunities to superior students. Average students–the kind recruited into MBRS–benefit as much as or more than their academically better prepared peers. Their classwork doesn't seem to suffer from time devoted to research. In fact, it often improves because of supportive relationships in the lab, and the increased interest in science generated by research.

Indeed, some undergraduates regard their research team as surrogate family. One student in biochemistry reported that the laboratory and his research group were a "place to go" after class, one where he could "talk chemistry." Before entering the MBRS program he returned to the barrio to "hang out" with friends; now the lab has become his hangout. Students often find a role model-mentor in a more advanced classmate. In one instance, the role model turned out to be a precocious thirteen-year-old female who came to Cal State LA at age nine under an early admissions program. Her discipline and intensity about her work, even as a preteen, so impressed a twenty-seven-year-old male Hispanic student that he freely admits that she was his inspiration.

As a result of its many successes and its willingness to give college dropouts from other schools another chance, chemistry-biochemistry is becoming the department of choice for minority science students. This sentiment is voiced by Carcy Chan, professor of chemistry at East Los Angeles Community College. She is director and principal investigator of one of the two MBRS programs at two-year colleges in the United States. Chan readily admits that even though her two-year chemistry graduates may qualify for UC (to earn B.A.s), she encourages them to go to Cal State LA.

Her reasons echo those of Cal State LA students themselves: a caring faculty that pays attention to minority students' needs; the MBRS and MARC programs which provide the funds needed for them to go on in science; and a feeling of being at home. Finally, and at least as important, is that East LA students can go directly into laboratory research as juniors before they complete coursework in the major. When these students apply to graduate school with a total of three or four years of research behind them, they have a leg up on their peers.

MBRS Students

In assessing the MBRS program our interviewer met with a number of MBRS students at Cal State LA, and several graduates working for advanced degrees. Many fit Dudley Herschbach's model of "long-distance runners" as opposed to the "sprinters" who Herschbach believes are favored by undergraduate science as it is currently structured and taught.[16] As if to prove the point, we found a master's student in Andreoli's lab, an American-born Asian twenty-six years old who, despite a high school science award, has been an erratic performer. He is typical of minority students who are not ready for graduate school immediately after earning a B.S. A Japanese-American professor at UC-Davis recommended him for a one- or two-year stint in Andreoli's lab to help him find direction. As part of his MBRS requirement he has had to take additional (undergraduate) courses, maintain a laboratory work schedule, and write a weekly report. He hopes to begin a Ph.D. in

---

[16] Herschbach, as quoted in *They're Not Dumb, They're Different: Stalking the Second Tier* (Tucson, Ariz.: Research Corporation, 1990), p. 61.

molecular genetics or a Ph.D.-M.D. program after the master's degree.

As this student sees it, MBRS gave him a second chance to develop good laboratory skills, to learn more biochemistry, and (if he performs well for Andreoli) "get another professional chemist in my camp." He also appreciates the salary–without which he would have had to get some other kind of paying job–the small research group, the individual attention, and the flexibility of the program. During one term, for example, he signed up for two sections of organic chemistry which he had taken before but never mastered. He thought the extra exposure to two different instructors would help the material sink in.

Another student in Andreoli's group is a Hispanic male, a senior in his second year of MBRS. He began his undergraduate career at a private four-year liberal arts college on a partial scholarship, but felt out of place and left after one year. When he arrived at Cal State LA, he "somehow met Andreoli" and decided to try biochemistry. As one of four children of a family on welfare, the MBRS salary is essential for him, he comments. After presenting a poster at a local meeting he concluded that "in science the work is more important than the color of your skin." He is now thinking about graduate school.

One senior MBRS student working in Tom Onak's research group is considering a graduate program in pharmacy or chemistry. A Mexican-American and the first in his family to go to college, he benefited from better than average science teaching at a small Catholic high school. He was recruited for the MBRS by Tony Fratiello, ever on the lookout for promising students. Two years later the student was able to present a paper before a local group and a poster at an ACS regional meeting. Both experiences "reinforced my commitment to a career in science," he says.

Another student of Mexican-American descent in Andreoli's lab graduated from MBRS and is now in the master's program at Cal State LA. An articulate, athletic young man and a good student at a local high school in the barrio, he earned a scholarship to Syracuse University, where he completed two years. Family problems brought him back home and he completed a B.S. at Cal State LA. Eager to continue study for a master's degree, he decided to hone his laboratory skills by staying on in Andreoli's lab. He described the experience of being part of a research group as a "critical factor in developing the discipline and enthusiasm needed to succeed in science."

A twenty-nine-year-old Asian-American female chose Cal State LA for a post-baccalaureate year because she wanted to work with Phoebe Dea. She had not been encouraged to consider graduate school at the private college from which she graduated with a "B" average. What she noticed right away was that, although the faculty-student ratio was no lower than at the private college, at Cal State LA "the students were always in the lab, working all kinds of odd hours." During her time at Cal State LA she delivered two papers at professional meetings, one a poster presentation at an ACS meeting in Washington, D.C., the other a talk on ethanol-phospholipid interaction (using NMR) in Miami, Florida. In both instances, she was prepared by Phoebe Dea and her lab mates in ways she has never encountered since. She was taught techniques for preparing a talk that would make her look professional. Once the slides were ready, she had to rehearse her paper orally in front of her fellow students and Phoebe Dea until she "got it right." Now completing a Ph.D. in chemistry at UCLA, this student says that

> If I had to list one aspect of the MBRS program important to me, it was traveling and giving the talks .... You stayed in the same hotel with people whose work you had read about . . . and the talks prepared me for all the talks I would have to give in my Ph.D. program.

Ray Garcia's lab attracts students whose interest is in research that touches on medical aspects of biochemistry. One Mexican-American young man in the group, now in his late twenties, was left to fend for himself as a teenager when his mother, a single parent, returned to Mexico. For a long time he had hoped to become a successful professional boxer, and had tried out for the 1984 Olympics both in LA and Mexico. By 1987 he finally abandoned this goal and transferred from LA City College, where he had been a part-time student, to Cal State LA where, as a full-time student, he was attracted to science. He has since presented work on the effect of jojoba oil on cholesterol levels in rabbits at a number of meetings. Membership in the MBRS research group and travel with the team helped him get over the feeling that he was an outsider, and gave him confidence that there is a "place for me in science."

Minority Access to Research Careers (MARC)

The presence of MBRS at Cal State LA has helped attract other programs intended to draw minority students to science. Minority Access to Research Careers (MARC) was started jointly in chemistry-biochemistry and biology in 1978, and is directed by Carlos Gutierrez. Like the MBRS, MARC is designed to produce students who can compete in graduate programs leading to Ph.D. degrees in the biomedical sciences. MARC is smaller than MBRS and is an honors program with a target population of high-performing (GPA 3.0 or above) undergraduates. Currently there are ten junior and senior minority students in

MARC, which has graduated forty-two students over its twelve-year history on campus.

At present, the program is funded at $200,000 per year by the National Institute of General Medical Sciences of the NIH. A MARC fellow receives a "stipend" (not a salary) of $6,500 per year plus registration, tuition, and compensation for school-related expenses. An additional $1,500 is available for laboratory supplies and travel. The fellowship usually covers the students' junior and senior years. Since it involves year-round research, students are encouraged to participate in off-site summer programs. A seminar series is also run in conjunction with MBRS and attendance is mandatory. Since MARC students write an honors thesis on their research, their skills and experience, Gutierrez contends, are comparable to those of M.S. graduates. Indeed, MARC student fellows have coauthored forty-one publications in refereed journals with faculty mentors, and have made over 100 presentations at scientific meetings.

Graduating MARC fellows are eligible to compete for NIH predoctoral fellowships in the amount of $8,500 annually, which can be used at any institution they select (the institution receives $2,000 as an additional bonus). Thus, when applying to graduate schools, MARC students have flexibility and built-in attractiveness that few other graduating seniors in science can match. They are, as Gutierrez says, "right up there with the best of them in every sense of the term."

Even though MARC fellows are academically talented, they share with MBRS students the same scarcity of resources and, in some cases, low self-esteem. Many have led sheltered, provincial lives in the inner city, having virtually no contact with scientists. They are grateful for the chance to venture far from home to attend scientific meetings and do summer research. Because of their high grade-point average and their laboratory experience, they are much sought after for summer programs at universities and other research laboratories.

Often, summer research takes them to an entirely different cultural setting. Recall that these students are, without exception, residents of Los Angeles and often limited, in their experience, to a very particular milieu. So when one Hispanic female from biologist Betsy Peitz' lab at Cal State LA was invited to join a research group at the Jackson Biological Laboratory in Bar Harbor, Maine in the summer of 1990, she was at first reluctant to go but, encouraged by Gutierrez and Peitz, accepted the appointment. At a post-summer meeting of MARC students the follow-ing fall, she described herself as having been at first overwhelmed by the beauty of New England, by the luxurious accommodations (from her point of view) in a former mansion in Bar Harbor, and by the fact that the lab mates in her working group were from prestigious Eastern colleges like Princeton and Harvard. The bottom line for MARC director Gutierrez, however, was that she proved herself to be as competent as they, and completed her assigned project in genetics with distinction. Best of all, she found out for herself how really good and how very well trained she was. Her fellow students in the MARC program seemed to profit from her experience too, and underlined the importance of these exchanges.

Like MBRS students, MARC students are encouraged to present their work at professional and student gatherings arranged by NIH for its fellows. In 1989-90, there were ninety MBRS and MARC student trips in total, some to a combined MBRS-MARC symposium in Nashville, Tennessee, some to the ACS national meeting in Hawaii. MBRS and MARC students also presented talks at the SACNAS (Society for the Advancement of Chicanos and Native Americans in Science) meeting in Costa Mesa, California.

The interaction at campus meetings of MARC and MBRS students reflects what makes the minority student programs at Cal State LA succeed. A male Hispanic senior who works in Phoebe Dea's analytical biochemistry lab discusses his calorimetry study of the effects of ethanol on phosphatidylethanolamine as it was presented at the Nashville meeting; a chemistry student describes his thrill at having the paper he presented at that same meeting submitted for publication. Both students talk of the rewards of travel and of presenting papers in a public forum. And they are not alone. Five other MARC students gave papers that same academic year.

At such a meeting, Gutierrez assures his students again and again that they are as capable as anyone studying anywhere. At this particular meeting he reminds them that the deadline for applying for the next GRE exam is coming soon; also that applications for graduate school are due. He, Fratiello, and Garcia are available for consultation, but the students must be prepared to "edit multiple drafts" before submitting a final version.

Not all MARC students are headed for research. Medicine is a powerful magnet for able, ambitious students, the first of their generation to enter college. But some will enlarge their vision to include research and even teaching. One black female, working on an enzyme problem in Scott Grover's lab, wanted to pursue medicine as early as high school, where she was one of fifteen black students in a graduating class of 200. To further her career interest, she spent 100 hours in a "career links" program at Livermore Hospital and enrolled at CSU Hayward, where she stayed but one year. As a transfer student at Cal State LA, she participated in both MARC and MBRS and presented papers at meetings in Washington, D.C., Canada (American Physiological Society), and New Orleans (FASEB). She is now headed for medical school, having a firm acceptance from a prestigious Eastern school in her pocket.

Other Programs

The faculty is ever vigilant in its search for new grants for minority programs. The RIMI program (Research Improvement in Minority Institutions) ran at Cal State LA from 1986 to 1990, funded ten students, and has been renewed for 1991 to 1994. Support for undergraduate honors students may be found in the project grants for faculty research made by such organizations as Research Corporation or the ACS-PRF. A program called Research Experiences for Undergraduates (REU), funded by the NSF, provides ten students with summer stipends for research in biology and chemistry. The program targets minority students as early as their sophomore year.

Grant-seeking is but one constant activity undertaken by Cal State LA faculty; another is identifying potential science students from local high schools. The department has an extensive network of contacts in area high schools and community colleges, and it recruits students for precollege summer research programs. Most will select more prestigious campuses in the UC system, but Cal State LA gives them a launch pad regardless.[17]

There are also support services for minority students. The Health Careers Opportunity Program (HCOP) funded by HHS provides assistance to students applying to health professional schools. The Minority Science Program (MSP) identifies and assists freshman minority students before they can be recruited into either MBRS or MARC. MSP is part of a system-wide initiative called ACCESS, to assist students in making the transition from high school to college. It provides tutorial assistance in biology, mathematics, physics, and chemistry under the direction of Ray Garcia (chemistry-biochemistry) and Margaret Jefferson (biology).

Conclusion

There is much to be learned from MBRS and MARC and from "affirmative education" as it is practiced at Cal State LA. The emphasis on undergraduate research has resulted in impressive numbers of graduates who have continued in Ph.D. and other professional programs

---

[17] Among these are SEED (Summer Educational Experience for the Disadvantaged), funded by the ACS.

at institutions of the first rank. That a significant number of those students are minority students, not all with high GPAs at the outset, and most in need of financial assistance to continue as full-time students, makes those numbers even more remarkable.

With sufficient resources, the success experienced by Cal State LA and the Department of Chemistry-Biochemistry over the past twenty years could be duplicated elsewhere. A university administration must cooperate, providing release time for faculty and funding for instrumentation. But the benefits to the host institution are many: increased faculty productivity, loyalty to their alma mater from successful minority graduates in science, and—given the discouraging statistics quoted at the beginning of this chapter—a grateful nation. The point is that so long as there is "affirmative education" at the college level, everything need not close down for minority seventeen-year-olds, however badly they have been served by their precollege education in mathematics and science. Dedicated teaching, access to research, salaries and stipends, opportunities for travel, and constant encouragement can compensate. In the long run, it may be more efficient to engage students at an earlier stage; but at present it is more likely that minority students will be recruited to science by programs like MBRS and MARC at the college level.

Indeed, it is not just minority students who are thriving at Cal State LA. During the 1988-89 academic year, the school ranked third among the twenty campuses in the CSU system in dollars awarded in external grants and contracts per full-time equivalent students. Still, the programs described in this chapter are always at risk. During the 1980s, NIH funding for both MBRS and MARC was frozen, and only in June 1991, for the first time in a decade, were there salary and stipend increases for participating students nationwide. Cal State LA has reason to believe that additional funding will continue to be available from a variety of sources to support MBRS and MARC. But no one can be sure. "Take away our funding," says former chemistry-biochemistry chairman Don Paulson, "and we're dead."

This chapter, more than any other, results from the work of a rapporteur. Sylvia Horowitz conducted all but a few of the interviews, compiled and updated information, and provided insight into, and interpretation of, the history and current activities of chemistry-biochemistry at Cal State LA.

10
Teaching Teachers
UCSD Revisited

W e have been looking at the role of the university in training scientists for the next generation. What is its role in training teachers of science? The temptation is to say that scientists are obligated first to the advancement of science; second, to the training of their graduate students; and third, to the education of undergraduates. The tendency has been to leave the training of precollege science teachers to education specialists.

What this means is that as colleges and universities are currently structured, science and "science education" are artificially disjoined. This is not entirely the fault of the science community. Ever since the rise of Deweyan philosophy in America, teachers, particularly teachers of young children, have been certified in pedagogy. So a thorough background in science is often sacrificed to "science methods" courses. As a consequence, more than half of the teachers of high school science have not majored in the subject they teach. Of the nation's one million elementary school teachers, only one in three has had a college chemistry course and only one in five a course in college physics.[1] *Can* anything be done about this? *Should* anything be done about this? Is there a role in teacher education, particularly elementary teacher education, for the great research universities?

Paul Saltman, former vice-chancellor of the University of California, San Diego (UCSD), research biochemist and popular teacher of the biology of nutrition course, thinks that there is. A science education activist, he is appalled, as he puts it, that the research universities have not only "abandoned the teaching of their own undergraduates, but public education (K-12) as well."[2] Saltman first turned his attention to teacher training in response to a mid-1980s demand to retrain teachers in

---

[1] 1985-1986 National Survey of Science and Mathematics Education conducted for NSF by the Research Triangle Institute, quoted in "Precollege Science and Mathematics Education," pp. 20 and 26.

[2] Quotations from personal interviews with Paul Saltman.

science and mathematics. Owing to a shift in demographics, San Diego County found itself with too few science and math teachers and too many (with tenure) in other areas. The challenge was to retrain some fifty "cross-over" teachers (grades seven to twelve) through intensive two-summer programs in science. The challenge for Saltman: What to teach them? How to teach them? Who to teach them?

UCSD does not offer degrees in education and has no school or department of education.[3] So Saltman had to create a science education team made up of research scientists and local master teachers of school science. Conspicuously absent were professors of education. He drew on UCSD faculty scientists to teach the science content and a husband-and-wife science-teaching team, Bob and Melanie Dean, from the public schools to run the afternoon laboratories. Mary Walshok, the energetic dean of extension at UCSD, offered the flexible administrative shelter of the continuing education department. The Deans provided direct access to the teachers and their schools. Together with Saltman, the team constituted a diverse group of people with different affiliations and skills.

Phase One: Retraining Cross-Over Teachers

From the beginning, Saltman laid down his "conditions:" first, the project had to involve the top faculty of his institution, "world-class scientists" who, as Saltman puts it, specialize in "knowing and loving their subject." Second, the teacher education model to be developed had to be exportable; other institutions should be able to duplicate it. Third, the project had to involve (at all stages) local educators, teachers, and administrators.

By 1984 he had a program working. In its first design, fifty teachers enrolled in two six-week summer programs that included chemistry, physics, biology, earth sciences, and astronomy. Five or six of the best faculty in these fields from UCSD gave morning lecture-demonstrations; afternoons were spent in a laboratory-like atmosphere learning to translate new knowledge into the curriculum the teachers would employ. For the afternoon sessions Bob and Melanie Dean recruited experienced science teachers from local schools as instructor-facilitators. Not just a

---

[3] Teacher Education Program (TEP) is the only "education" unit on campus, with a mandate to develop, in cooperation with the San Diego County School District, postbaccalaureate programs in certification of middle and senior high school teachers, particularly, but not exclusively, in science and mathematics. Graduates of UCSD with standard majors in science and mathematics are invited to take three summers and two afternoons per week of coursework in "education," all the while working part-time as apprentice teachers in the district.

summer experience to be forgotten, the program had teachers come back one Saturday per month during the school year for lectures on "contemporary issues in science" and for field trips.

With substantive lectures in science in the mornings and curricular applications in the afternoon, Saltman's model essentially eliminated traditional teacher training in science, namely "science methods." To the extent that pedagogy showed up at all, it did so as an application of the science learned. Since there were no professional pedagogues on the team, the informal treatment of pedagogy was not a problem. The working assumption was that once informed about science and provided with materials, the cross-over teachers could figure out how to *teach* science on their own.

The cross-over program continued for two years. In Saltman's view, the program was good but not great.

> The teachers, even those under duress, got something out of it. They improved their science literacy. They felt better about science. They knew how to look things up in a textbook. They had a whole set of experiments to take back to their schools. And they felt more comfortable going into a science classroom than they would have . . . . Above all, they felt comfortable with the [university] science faculty, perhaps for the first time.

The problem, as Saltman sees it, was that there was no way for the program to reach more than the fifty teachers enrolled; there was no "amplifier," as he puts it. Further, they were rushed through so much in so little time, they could not "embrace science with a passion;" they accepted it. They absorbed it as if their lessons were intellectual nutrients, but not (Paul Saltman is a nutritional biochemist) as if they constituted a feast.

By the time the cross-over program was completed, Paul Saltman had spent two years on the advisory panel to NSF's Science and Engineering Education (now Education and Human Resources) Directorate. He came to believe, as does NSF, that the "science education crisis" did not originate in junior and senior high school, but in elementary school. Could the cross-over program be modified to improve the science competence of elementary school teachers?

Phase Two: Educating Elementary Teachers

Phase two was designed to retrain elementary teachers. This time Saltman "spaced out the learning curve," making the program more intense and longer (three summers) in duration. Using the format tested on the cross-over teachers, mornings featured UCSD faculty presenting substantive material, and afternoons were spent providing practical experience to illustrate general concepts. The afternoon sessions featured experiments teachers could perform in the classroom.

One hundred elementary school teachers were selected to spend three summers and many school-year Saturdays in a program which Saltman hoped would proceed from familiar biology (the first summer) through earth sciences, the cosmos, oceanography, and meteorology (the second summer) and finally, in the third summer, to the subjects he believed elementary teachers feared most, chemistry and physics.

He was correct in his perceptions of teachers' attitudes toward physics and chemistry. One teacher told our interviewer that if physics and chemistry had come first, "many of us would have dropped out of the program right away!"

When you listen to Paul Saltman talk about the program, you realize that, in addition to science content, he intended that an imaginative attitude and approach to science be conveyed in those morning lectures. To accomplish this, he encouraged his university faculty to construct their own syllabus, and to present topics creatively and in whatever order they chose. Given the vertical structure of science, the fact that topics are logically nested inside one another, this was a most unusual organization. Scientists believe–and their textbooks and courses reflect it–that there is an internal structure to each discipline and that teaching an array of different topics does not reflect the methods of science. Saltman was willing to have his instructors depart from traditional scope and sequence, urging them only to "tell them why you love your subject and what you know about it."

Teacher candidates were offered stipends of $2,400 for the full three-year program, books, materials, and equipment, as well as units towards the master's degree and science teachers' certification. With all these benefits and the possibility of achieving some kind of "comfort zone" in science, it was expected that hundreds of teachers from San Diego County's numerous school districts would respond to a mailing sent to 6,000. In fact, the elaborate selection procedure which had been set up to achieve a balance of teachers never had to be put to use. For 100 budgeted openings, only 102 teachers applied, so the program took all of them.[4]

Saltman built an "amplifier" into the program. Even 100 retrained elementary teachers wouldn't make a dent in one local district, so each teacher had to agree (à la Mao Tse-tung) to teach ten colleagues in her or his home school. And each local principal would authorize the time as

---

[4] After three years, seventy-five of the original 102 were still with the program, and all but a few of those who dropped out had either moved away or left teaching altogether. Their places were filled as the program progressed.

part of a contract with Saltman's program. Again, professional science educators were not involved. The afternoon sessions were led by what Saltman calls "on-line" science teachers.

With $940,000 from NSF for the three-year program and $50,000 raised from private sources, the UCSD Science Institute for Elementary Teachers began. Based on Saltman's view that the problem in elementary science resides not in the curriculum, but in "the scarcity of knowledgeable and understanding teachers," the program's goal was not just to increase the teachers' knowledge of science, but to empower each with "a love of science." His view of their needs was confirmed by many of the teachers themselves. One, Terry Early, admitted that prior to the program her greatest fear had been that her students would ask questions she could not answer. Like most elementary school teachers (only 8 percent of the participating teachers–4 percent nationally–had ever taken a college physical science course), her science background was limited.[5]

> I relied on classroom textbooks and prepared workbooks for many of my lessons. Science was my least favorite subject. The UCSD program has changed all that. More than anything, I have gained self-confidence. I see now that I was simply memorizing facts with no real understanding of scientific principles.

Another teacher, George Olguin, said he used to think his obligation was to make sure "the kids got a lot of facts," but was uncomfortable with that approach. After participating in the institute, he now finds ways to have them "experience science."

The program directors believe that Olguin's conversion is typical. Teachers who used to teach science twenty minutes a week now claim to be spending forty minutes a day on it. "Teachers are excited. Their students are excited. The institute has given them the knowledge, tools, and confidence to teach the subject," says Saltman. Now the questions are: Will the excitement last? Will the teachers maintain their new level of competency by adding to their knowledge on their own? And can the program, indeed, be exported?

Teaching Elementary Teachers (Not So) Elementary Science

Some of the institute faculty had never taught an undergraduate course before, much less a course for elementary teachers. They were selected from the greater UCSD science community because Saltman

---

[5] The following quotes are taken from an article about the program by Sharon Taylor which appeared in *UCSD Perspectives.*

thought they could, as research scientists, convey to the teachers the "experience" of science, as well as the principles of their discipline. Among others the institute's faculty included Walter Munk from the Scripps Institute of Oceanography; geologist Joseph Curray; meteorologist Richard Somerville; astronomer Harding Smith; physics professor Sheldon Schultz; and biochemistry professor Russell Doolittle. Doolittle's two-week offering in chemistry was the last minicourse in the series, and was monitored for this study.

Teaching Chemistry[6]

Russ Doolittle's goal for his two-week introductory chemistry course was to give the teachers a feel for what chemists do. He didn't fret much about the topics he was going to cover, for Saltman gave him free rein. The purpose, in any case, was not so much to "deposit" information as to demonstrate that "even the most baffling and mysterious [things in science] can be known." Although there were assignments in two texts,[7] Doolittle relied on them mainly for charts and tables, providing the continuing narrative himself.

Doolittle began with the periodic table, simple reaction equations, the historical derivation of atomic weights, and exercises involving combining ratios. In succeeding classes he explained the basic concepts of electricity and the nature of compounds and solution chemistry. He went into detail about a few important experiments which revealed the nature of the atom (Thomson's and Millikan's), a little about the light spectrum, X rays, and radioactivity. He ended his minicourse with what he called the "modern understanding of atomic structure." In eleven two-hour lectures (August 2-16, 1990), Doolittle exposed the class to increasingly complex descriptions of atomic structure to give them an understanding of how and why elements combine to form compounds.

Each two-hour lecture featured a large amount of sophisticated material, but what made it accessible to the teachers was Doolittle's conceptual narrative and the downplaying of the problem solving found in traditional courses. He started with the simplest ideas and then moved

---

[6] This section is based largely on journals kept by two participant-observers, Debbie Ashcraft and Therese Flaningam, and on a set of observations by P.A. Moore, one of the program's administrators. Jacqueline Raphael, an assistant to this project, listened to the twenty-two hours of taped lectures to get a record of the content of Doolittle's minicourse in chemistry and for illustrations of his teaching.

[7] Theodore L. Brown, et al., *Chemistry, The Central Science*, 4th ed. (Englewood Cliffs, N.J.: Prentice Hall, 1988), prologue, chaps. 1, 4, 5, 6, 7, 8, 20; and Paul G. Hewitt, *Conceptual Physics*, 6th ed. (Boston: Little Brown, 1988), chaps. 10, 14, and 16.

on, developing students' knowledge base until they could grasp more complex concepts.[8]

Doolittle's Approach

Doolittle's approach to the teaching of chemistry, he told his teachers, would be dualistic. "We're going to dance back and forth," he said, "between the history of the unraveling and solving of chemical problems and the modern scientist's understanding of the discipline." Indeed, he attempted to reconstruct the *logic of discovery*, for this body of knowledge called chemistry has taken a long time to assemble. "There was tremendous confusion among chemists most of the time." What made some better scientists than others was not "genius or great math skills, but curiosity, persistence, and fanaticism—a desperate need to know the answer to a question," Doolittle said.

In "unveiling" new concepts he traced the inductive reasoning of scientists like Dalton, Avogadro, and Rutherford, asking teachers how *they* would have approached a particular mystery. "How did the first chemists determine the exact composition of oxygen and hydrogen in simple compounds, such as water?" he asked one day, and proceeded to tell them. Or, "Why do some elements want to donate or share electrons, while others don't want to play the game at all?"

One technique Doolittle employed was to start each day's class with a review of what had been covered the day before. Another was his explanation of the importance of new material. "Much of chemistry has been taught phenomenologically," he would say, "as if simply stating that the addition of X to Y produces Z would explain what is most important, namely *why*."

Many new terms came into play in solution chemistry—ions, cations, anions—and Doolittle suggested mnemonic aids and provided as many general rules as possible to help the teachers remember chemical principles. The basic building blocks of matter—charged particles—and the "magic" of the periodic table, arranged according to properties of elements, were revisited to help explain new material. Perhaps the teachers would find occasion to explain to their students (even elementary pupils) how much of a resource the periodic table is.

Problem solving was downplayed but not ignored. "There is no way,"

---

[8] Doolittle's "syllabus," distributed on the first day to the teachers, listed the following lecture topics: (1) "What is Chemistry?;" (2) "The Periodic Table;" (3) "Atomic Structure;" (4) "All About Light;" (5) "Chemical Bonds;" (6) "Counting in Chemistry;" (7) "The Gas Laws Again;" (8) "All About Water;" (9) "Why Do Things Happen?;" (10) "Faraday's Laws;" and (11) "Oxidation-Reduction."

Doolittle told the teachers, "that I can teach you enough about composition of compounds without going over combining ratios and balancing chemical equations." He spent a good deal of time explaining the ideas behind Avogadro's number, for example, because it describes "how everything got counted." He wanted his teachers to write down Avogadro's number, understand it, "believe it, even." He would talk them through problems such as one involving the atomic weight of an unknown element. "Imagine that ten grams of an oxide, XO, is heated and the oxygen released into the atmosphere. Six grams of X remain. What is element X?"

Urging teachers to *think about* their problems qualitatively before setting out to solve them, and to use intuition as well as formulas, Doolittle pointed out that students particularly adept at mathematics often skip *thinking steps* and go straight for an answer. He wanted teachers to aim for a deeper understanding of the concepts in chemistry and to persist.

"Active learning" involves both highs and lows, he told them. "Sometimes you'll say, 'I get it'. Other times, 'I'm completely baffled.' Both are part of the process."

Pedagogy by Indirection

None of Saltman's "world-class scientists" were supposed to teach "science methods," but their pedagogy could not go unnoticed by teachers who were schooled in the subject of *teaching*. One observer, P.A. Moore, who holds a doctorate in education and who studied the impact of the Saltman program, described Doolittle's teaching style:

> On the first day, he asked participants to think about the nature of the chemical world from the point of view of an early Greek or Roman. How much did they know? How did they know it? And from this point on, he took his students on a tour of chemistry, building from early insights and moving to the complexities of atomic energy.

Many of the participants volunteered to P.A. Moore that Russ Doolittle "modeled good teaching behavior."

> He engaged the participants by asking questions. Recognizing that proximity is a means of encouragement, he would move up and down the aisles to engage as many of them as possible. He often paused in reflection and invited the participants to do likewise. When moving from layperson's language to chemical symbolism, he would announce, "We're going into the symbolic mode now," and he would then go to the chalkboard and write down the chemical notations.

On occasion, he would pose a question, invite everyone to write an answer, and then walk up and down the aisles checking responses, giving praise for right responses (or letting those teachers go to coffee break before the others), and suggesting improvements for wrong ones.

Moore thinks it was Doolittle's "positive attitude" and his "nonthreatening manner" that stimulated class discussion. Teachers asked questions freely and, Moore noticed, actively took notes. The modest increase in their scores on a pretest/posttest administered respectively in May and August 1990 affirmed this.[9] The teachers told Moore they particularly enjoyed their "hands-on" experience in the labs where they did experiments, applying concepts they had learned that morning. Saltman was determined to send them home with a "four-foot shelf" of lab materials, so that inadequate laboratory supplies would not be a problem for them when they tried to do these experiments for their pupils. In addition, he established a lending library of science supplies, materials, and resources for participants.

Participants' Observations

The daily journals kept by the two participant-observers affirm how Doolittle's teaching became a model for their own. One participant noted in her journal, "Saying something again and in a different way can make a great deal of difference. I need to remember this as I teach my own students." Equally important was that they began to "feel good" about chemistry. What they enjoyed was the privilege (their term) of being on a campus with the reputation of UCSD; of being "exposed" to professors of the quality of Doolittle and the others, and of "having the latest information in each field of science from plate tectonics to the Hubble space telescope." "I heard it from the horse's mouth," Therese Flaningam wrote in her final essay for this project, "and I understood it."

Therese Flaningam wanted "to know the history of basic chemistry," and to learn "to speak the language." She found Doolittle a "truly gifted teacher" who made it easier to learn the many new terms she confronted by explaining the derivations of the Latin names of the elements. After the first week, Flaningam wrote in her journal:

> I was not only learning chemistry, I was learning the methods
> and teaching techniques that work with students. I felt confi-

---

[9] Approximately 68 percent of the teachers showed an increase on the posttest scores; 12 percent maintained the same score; and 20 percent showed a decrease. The mean increase was three percentage points.

dent and I was beginning to *enjoy* chemistry. Even though I didn't know all the answers, I realized that things would become clearer later on; that much of science is trial and error—just what I was doing.

Later she added,

Scientists in the nineteenth century puzzled over how the elements combine to form different compounds. Dr. Doolittle had *us* puzzle over it as well. What does the periodic table mean? Thinking and predicting seem to be the keys to science.

Flaningam gathered many other insights from playing student ("A very humbling experience... being on the other side of the desk will help me when I return to the classroom") that she would consider using as a teacher. She was impressed with Doolittle's use of the discovery method, for example, though she acknowledged in her notes that it takes time to have students *think* through the logic. She felt *she* could "hang onto" a concept longer knowing how it was derived, but recognized that in applying discovery to her own class, she could lose students whose "light bulbs" don't all go on at the same time.

Flaningam and her fellow teachers were impressed with Doolittle's metaphors. He used the analogy of a hotel (atom) with floors (orbitals), rooms (sublevels), and roomers (electrons) to illustrate the quantum mechanical model of the atom. In explaining the reactivity of sodium, he invited the class to consider the one lone roomer in a sodium atom on the third floor. Flaningam thought the notion that inert gases have "no vacancy" was clever. She was amazed that she "finally got a glimpse of the meaning of the periodic table" which (for her) was like solving the mystery of the Rosetta stone.

Debbie Ashcraft, voted "Teacher of the Year" in her San Diego school, began teaching at age thirty. A Spanish major who later received a master's degree in education, she had been teaching for twelve years when she enrolled in the UCSD institute. Though she remembered having a "keen interest in science, especially laboratory science, in junior high school," she did "terribly" in a chemistry course in those years. Thereafter she became, by her own admission, a science avoider. Even after returning to school in her late twenties, a mature and much more serious student, she continued to avoid science, so much so that in her words, "My science program [at the school where she taught] was a disaster.... I truly dreaded teaching science and hated the preparation."

So why did she enroll in the UCSD program? The money, the thirty "free" credits toward advancement, and her problems with teaching science.

Ashcraft was at first skeptical of Doolittle's teaching style–the text-book assignments and the lectures were not always in step. But in time Doolittle became for her the "person she could learn chemistry from," perhaps the only one. She was confused when Doolittle explained something differently than the book; or when lectures and reading assignments didn't match. She needed to talk through her problems and was uncomfortable struggling alone. Once, after getting much-needed help from a classmate (on combining ratios), she wished there had been more peer discussion in class. But the time to spend on chemistry at home–time she knew she really needed–was simply not available to her. She claimed to have more confidence in chemistry as a result of Doolittle's teaching, but she wasn't sure she could continue to learn it on her own.

Ashcraft needed variety in "delivery systems." She appreciated being led through visual descriptions of experiments, bonding angles, and chemical relationships. Like many of her own pupils, she noted that she is the kind of learner who gains most from *activity*. Labs helped her understand in greater depth the concepts covered in morning lectures and gave her a "true life" feeling about science. "We got to do all the things that I was cheated out of as a child and I felt all the wonderment and excitement of discovery that I should have experienced years ago."

She also appreciated the fact that Doolittle wrote out formulas on the chalkboard in words, and was happiest when Doolittle's logic corresponded with her own. Just before a fire alarm sent the teachers out onto the lawn one morning, Doolittle was telling them about Rutherford's discovery of the atomic nucleus. This is how the drama unfolded for Debbie Ashcraft:

> He gave us the historical background of X rays and radioactivity, which I found very interesting. I learned the reason for naming alpha, beta, and gamma particles. He piqued our curiosity by promising to tell us why Rutherford was *surprised* by his experiments.

The fire alarm was not enough to kill a lively discussion which continued on the lawn. The surprise for Rutherford had been that most of the atomic mass was concentrated in a very small central core of the atom which he then named the nucleus.

> So the nucleus of the atom was far away from the electrons. I . . . could see where [Doolittle] was heading. . . . Having additional electrons in the nucleus wouldn't work.

She was thinking on her own and trying to anticipate explanations. And that, for Debbie, was significant. To celebrate, she ends her journal entry for that day with the words, "Great stuff!" Debbie was getting more problems right and becoming more articulate in her comments about chemistry.

Still, when the instructor was forced to "step up the pace," Debbie Ashcraft got lost. This made her appreciate how carefully he was pacing his lectures generally. She also noticed his ability to "read our faces" during the presentation of particularly confusing matter and marveled at his willingness to employ the "class-involving techniques" she uses with her elementary children. Doolittle was the first college professor Ashcraft had ever had who appeared to be *aware* of teaching techniques. "What works for kids also works for adults," she noticed with some surprise. The reverse–what works for adults might work for kids– was the whole point of the program.

Pedagogy at its Most Experiential

Although institute instructors each selected and organized the topics they taught, there were common elements in the way they responded to the needs of science-deficient teachers. Even though Saltman did not dictate pedagogy or curriculum, the instructors tried to make teachers feel comfortable with their respective disciplines and the individual language used in each. Specific topics were consciously supplemented with at least some glimpses of the "big picture." This, in turn, says Kathleen Grove, a non-participant observer who interviewed some of the teachers during Doolittle's class, made the teachers feel more competent in science.

One participating teacher told Grove the program had made her "science literate," by which she meant she came away with a sense of "where science is going." Although she realized "how much there is to know," she no longer felt helpless or obliged to know it all. Saltman's desire that his instructors communicate their passion for science also contributed to the overwhelmingly positive feeling experienced by many of the participants. It may have been humbling for some, but in the end teachers became excited about science, something many of them had never experienced before.

There is presently much debate about how to remedy elementary teachers' science deficiencies. One approach is characterized by a "less is more" philosophy: "Teach a few basic principles, in depth and well, and elementary teachers will learn how to educate themselves in science," says one school of thought. Another recommends an overview: "Give teachers a sense of where they're heading (and where they need to go to get help)." Neither philosophy was formally adopted by the institute's instructors. Saltman and his colleagues are not experts in "teaching

154

methods," nor much interested in that literature. Rather, they appear to have opted intuitively for the ultimate hands-on approach: don't tell teachers how to teach. Turn them into students and let them figure it out for themselves.

Indeed, participants in the institute program wanted to be treated like intelligent students and their frustrations, as well as their successes, reflect that fact. Stepping into the learner's shoes may have been the most useful aspect of the program. Teachers became increasingly self-conscious in their shifting roles. They were alternately students in a "difficult course," with new material coming at them every class hour, including homework assignments and tests, and they were also teachers, observing a master teacher cope with *their* deficiencies and resistance as they would eventually have to cope with their students'. Debbie Ashcraft reported in her journal with surprise that some of her fellow teachers were not doing their homework or attending lab sessions as conscientiously as she was. One wonders whether, as they experienced their own recalcitrance, these teachers did not think about ways of overcoming comparable resistance in their students. This is pedagogy at its most experiential. As Therese Flaningam reflects, "Chemistry is hard, but the difficulty is learning *how to learn* the subject, rather than the subject itself."

"Cloning" the Project

As early as 1989 the decision was made to try to clone the UCSD summer institute and to involve other California research universities in improving science teaching. Saltman was awarded $90,000 from NSF to support the development of "daughter projects." The first step was to invite research scientists from prospective schools to observe the UCSD summer institute. They came away impressed. David Deamer, professor of zoology at UC-Davis said of his visit, "As soon as you walked in the room, you saw something real happening to these people."

In 1990 six research universities submitted proposals to NSF for funding at the same level as Saltman's original program, $1 million per 100 teachers per institution over three years.[10] In each instance, the players included a research university (e.g., UC-Davis), a school district

[10] Locations and clients of proposed clone projects were: University of California-Davis (for teachers from the Sacramento School District); University of San Francisco (for teachers from the San Francisco School District); Stanford University (for teachers from the Palo Alto and San Jose School Districts); University of Southern California (for teachers from the Los Angeles Unified School District); University of Hawaii (for teachers from the entire island system); and University of California at Berkeley (for teachers from the Berkeley and part of the Oakland School Districts).

(e.g., Sacramento), and an accrediting department. If a university department of education was unwilling, another department, such as continuing medical education (as at the University of Hawaii), would do. Saltman's "conditions" were adopted by the six applicants: "world class" faculty for the morning lectures and local science teaching specialists for afternoon laboratory. The education professoriate was not asked to participate.

In Paul Saltman's vision, there were to be six great universities prepared to metamorphose elementary science education in a new framework. Two years later, NSF had funded projects at the University of Hawaii and at the University of San Francisco, and the Davis program was to be funded as well. Two of the six, Stanford and USC, were anticipating private funding.

Conclusion

How far can the Saltman model go? Already there are changes in the structure of the school year in certain parts of California which militate against summer training for teachers. In order to avoid building more schools, San Diego County, for example, has gone to year-round plant utilization which means that one-fourth of all elementary teachers are teaching in the summer. Enrichment programs of the kind offered by the UCSD summer institute, Saltman says, will henceforth have to be scheduled in the "interstices of teachers' time." In the interim, the leadership (even the name) of NSF's Science and Engineering Education Directorate has changed. New leadership brings with it new priorities and different models. Yet, without millions of dollars of *continuing* outside funding, institute clones–and the UCSD summer institute itself–are in jeopardy.

Not that the beneficial effects of Saltman's project are in doubt. In the past eighteen months, summer institute teachers have become valuable resource teachers in their schools, and there is evidence that they and their colleagues are spending more time teaching science than they ever did before. The California State Department of Education wants to use the Saltman model to promote the state's "new curriculum framework" in science and mathematics education. The fact that several states are now requiring *all* preservice teachers, elementary as well as secondary, to major in some discipline other than "education"–suggests that the idea of teaching *science* to elementary teachers instead of merely *science methods* is an idea whose time has come.

In a period of declining state revenues and growing competition for national funding, however, who will foot the bill even for programs that are successful? And how long will Paul Saltman and his friends be available to the summer institute? Program initiators experience burn-out. Research scientists may not be willing to continue the experiment year after year. The time may have come for the idea of teaching elementary teachers real science, but until and unless the program becomes part of the mainstream, it remains just that: an idea.

There are one million elementary school teachers in the United States, 80 percent or more of whom are inadequately trained in science. The profession experiences a 15 percent turnover rate, which means every six or seven years there will be another cohort of one million to retrain. At 100 teachers per $1 million program, the nation would have to fund 10,000 programs (and every six or seven years, 10,000 more). Thus, the projected cost of doing on a national scale what Paul Saltman did locally in San Diego is, at least, $10 billion, or twenty-five times the recently increased annual NSF budget for education and human resources. No one doubts that it is worthwhile to bring the nation's elementary school teachers to the point where they can adequately convey both the facts and the drama of science. But given the nation's other pressing priorities, how much is it worth? And at the expense of what else?

Saltman will say these figures do not take into account the "amplifier effect" of his program. If phase two of the institute accomplishes its aims, during the next three years 3,000 to 4,000 elementary teachers in San Diego County will have "directly or indirectly benefited from the program," as Saltman sees it. That is because the 102 teachers were given not just content knowledge and teaching strategies, but leadership training as well. The intention was to send them back to their home districts equipped to become teacher-trainers in turn. To make this possible, Saltman and the Deans arrange two-week institutes, and provide ongoing follow-up. And in fact, in the two years since the summer program came to an end, some (though not all) of the 102 have proved themselves capable of teaching elementary science to their colleagues; others are involved in science lesson-planning in their districts; still others are "peer-coaching" in their home schools. In a video report of phase two, most say they have gained skills, confidence, and credibility from their participation in the UCSD program. Best of all, they have made friends with their professors. Russ Doolittle and several other UCSD faculty have visited their schools and made themselves otherwise available to the teachers whose science anxiety they worked hard to dispel.[11]

---

[11] Taken from a talk Paul Saltman gave about the project at the Research Corporation's Science Partnerships Conference, Jan. 1991, published in *Highlights from Science Partnerships in Action*, Research Corporation, 1991, p.12.

What Paul Saltman and his colleagues set out to demonstrate at UCSD has been demonstrated. Some 102 "scared to death" elementary teachers can be reeducated in science and affect positively the *attitudes* of the children they teach. But how will programs like Saltman's become mainstreamed? And who will fight for revision of certification requirements in fifty states that allow those not educated in science to teach it? Who will battle the teachers' unions on the issue of differential pay for science specialists, without which the assignment of elementary teachers to the subjects they teach best is not realistic? In his summer institute Saltman was able to end run professional educators by giving his teachers continuing education credits and pay. How will it be possible to apply that model in preservice training? And, in the long run, mustn't we improve teachers' preservice education and raise certification standards so that remediation is not nearly so necessary?

In 1985, the National Science Board published a report that called upon institutions of higher education to shoulder more of the responsibility for precollege science and mathematics education.[12] The report urged colleges and universities to raise their admissions standards, increase the rigor of the curriculum that future teachers study, and put greater emphasis on disciplinary subjects. It called for fewer but more rigorous teacher education methods courses and for colleges and universities to recruit talented students into the teaching profession.

No one disputes these recommendations. The challenge is how to implement them!

---

[12] "Educating Americans for the 21st Century," prepared by the Commission on Precollege Education in Mathematics, Science and Technology, established by the National Science Board, 1985.

11
Conclusion
The Implementation Challenge

The primary barrier to reform is not
money, but will—which must be driven
by a compelling vision of what works.
—*Daniel F. Sullivan, Project Kaleidoscope*[1]

What can we learn from programs that succeed, and from programs that don't work as well as was intended? There will be some disagreement as to the meaning of the case studies reported here but some tentative conclusions can be drawn: first, change is not implemented by experts, but originates in local commitment and reallocation of resources at the midlevel of management–in the case of colleges and universities, the *department*. In fact the department is the unit of change. Second, money finds its way *directly* into instruction. One good use of it appears to be the support of faculty research which, in turn, supports and engages undergraduates; another is for improved laboratory equipment and instrumentation. Yet a third worthy expenditure is for what Luther Williams, NSF's assistant director for education and human resources, calls "post-performance rewards" for instructional units that do continuously improve. But most important, the case studies suggest that what we need to do above all else is collect information on how successful faculty support and manage improvement.

A hallmark of effective programs is that the process of reform is all-engaging. Ideas are solicited from faculty and implemented locally by the department. Where programs don't work, a creative loner is frequently found to be proceeding without internal support and commitment. Lasting change is occurring when everyone wants it, when there is a nearly universal buy-in. Despite the idiosyncracies of particular programs, when successful faculty speak about what they are accomplishing

---

[1] *What Works: Building Natural Science Communities*, Vol. II, Project Kaleidoscope, December 1991.

158

in the teaching and training of undergraduates, they speak with one voice. There is passion.

Why are they passionate? In many cases, the faculty themselves are first-generation scholars, brought to the professoriate by the GI Bill, National Defense Education Act fellowships, and Sputnik. They are grateful to their country for these opportunities, and they feel that their students, especially their minority students, are not very different from themselves. In other institutions, where such identification does not arise naturally, it is deliberately cultivated. In either case, the faculty seeks, creatively and at every juncture, to meet students' needs. Grading is personal and not mechanistic (occasional large classes notwithstanding); and competition between students tends to be de-emphasized. Where classes are small there is more intimacy between professor and class; less intimidation, less passivity in the classroom, a better sense of *community*.

The places where programs work are very often four-year state and private institutions which have no graduate students to draw on, and so are hungry for undergraduates to participate in faculty research. Research-oriented faculty are motivated to identify students as early as possible who can assist them in their laboratory. This means they pay a lot of attention to the first-year class. Faculty are competing with each other for undergraduates, and the undergraduates win. Where there is long-term outside funding for research, a program can be developed and sustained. At Cal State LA, as we have seen, there is an eighteen-year NIH funding record for faculty research involving undergraduates. There is no inevitable cut off of funds, and the money is being well spent. But at many institutions with successful programs, funding is entirely internal.

In places where programs work, department members are not waiting around for the traditional reward system to change, although there are some interesting moves afoot to redefine scholarship to give teaching more weight.[2] Deans and department chairs have discovered the power of the "little 'r'"– the small reward for work well done, the enabling reward so that things can be done a little better each time. The model, one faculty member tells me, is "Skinnerian. Find out what works and reward it." The process, says another, may require new kinds of money, money that enables: a line of credit, for example, assigned to a large course so that the professor can buy what he or she needs to make the teaching better; another research assistant to enable the professor to spend more time on teaching; additional grading staff (from the community if necessary) so

---

[2] Ernest L. Boyer, *The Condition of the Professoriate: Attitudes and Trends* (Lawrenceville, N.J.: Princeton University Press, 1989) See also Karl S. Pister, "Report to the University-wide Task Force on Faculty Rewards," Office of the President, University of California, Oakland, Calif., 1991.

that professors can ask the kinds of questions they'd like to ask but don't have time to grade; or money for extra lab spaces or travel.

Taken together, one can draw a tentative conclusion from all these examples. The model for science education reform is not an experimental model, not even a research model, but a *process model* that focuses attention continuously on every aspect of the teaching-learning enterprise, locally and in depth. To make cumulative improvement, there have to be feedback mechanisms in place so that one knows almost immediately–not just at the end of a course–that something is going wrong, that some of the students are losing confidence, that instruction is failing them. Once a problem is identified, a solution is sought, locally and fast. The Japanese call this process (as applied to industrial quality control) *Kai Zen*, meaning, literally, "change in the direction of the good." In programs that work, faculty members pay continuous attention to "what we teach, who we teach, and how we teach."[3]

When, during my several exchanges with Fort Lewis' chemistry department, I questioned the chairman about the process by which change was introduced and quality maintained, Jim Mills described his as a "strategic" department, not inclined to embark on major experimental teaching projects. Instead, he said, the faculty tries hard to judge which changes will work, given local conditions. "This means we must know who we are and who our students are." Their goal, you will recall (see page 49), is "to do a better job with our students each year," and there is general faculty opinion that they do.

SUNY Potsdam

Twenty years ago, just such a mix of tangibles and intangibles began to bear fruit in undergraduate mathematics at Potsdam College of the State University of New York (SUNY). Under the leadership of mathematician Clarence Stephens who had previously taught at Morgan State University, a historically black institution in the Maryland state system, a dual-degree program was established in which a student could obtain both B.A. and M.A. degrees in four years without summer school. But Stephens' agenda was more ambitious. He wanted to demonstrate to liberal arts students that anyone could succeed in mathematics. His strategy focused on excessive faculty concern about coverage of subject matter and academic standards; and inadequate institutional support for undergraduate teaching.[4]

---

[3] James Duderstadt, "Keynote Address," *The Freshman Year in Science and Engineering,* The Alliance for Undergraduate Education, University of Michigan conference, 1990, p. 6.

[4] Taken from Gloria F. Gilmer and Scott W. Williams, "An Interview with Clarence

Stephens found a faculty receptive to his ideas and under his steady stewardship they set about changing each of these conditions. The results, over more than two decades, have been spectacular. Of the 700 or so students who annually graduate, more than 10 percent graduate with a mathematics major, and more than half of these are women. During a run of five years in the 1980s (1984-1988), the percentage of math majors per graduating class ranged from 17 to 25, compared to a national average of between 1 and 2 percent. Only UCLA and the University of Illinois at Urbana produce more mathematics majors than Potsdam. On the basis of percentage of the graduating class who are math majors, however, Potsdam has consistently been unsurpassed. Even after stabilizing at 10 percent per class, SUNY Potsdam is sufficiently noteworthy to have been recognized for its outstanding program by the Mathematical Association of America.[5] There is no end in sight. The faculty remains completely committed under the leadership of Vasily Cateforis, who succeeded Stephens as chairman in 1987. That students are warmly welcomed and succeed at mathematics at SUNY Potsdam is so well known in high schools throughout the state that almost *half* of all the freshman classes elect calculus.

What is the secret of success at SUNY Potsdam? Not any particular curriculum or pedagogy, nor any add-on activities. Cheri Boyd, a graduate of the program who recently earned a Ph.D. in mathematics from the University of Rochester, remembers that ". . . most of the good stuff happened in the classroom."[6] Like Jim Mills of Fort Lewis, Stephens, Cateforis, and their colleagues firmly believe that "effective teaching is not independent of time and place," but must fit the local environment. At SUNY Potsdam instructors are free to choose their teaching methods; but along with that freedom comes faculty responsibility for results achieved.[7] As Stephens told an interviewer in 1989,

> While we recognize the importance of [curriculum and technology] in the improvement of mathematics education, [here] we focused on . . . changing the [view] of students, faculty, and academic administrators that mathematics is a subject which is impossible for most students to learn . . . . Once the faculty discovered that [they could teach] students how to reason about mathematical ideas, then the faculty became [more] interested in teaching [those skills] than in covering a lot of content . . . .

Stephens," UME *Trends*, AMS, MAA, SIAM, Vol. 2, No. 1, March 1990.

[5] *Recommendation for a General Mathematical Sciences Program*, Mathematical Association of America, 1981.

[6] Personal communication to the author.

[7] Gilmer and Williams, "An Interview with Clarence Stephens."

Sacrifice of coverage turns out not to be a major problem. Observers note that by the time SUNY Potsdam students are seniors, many can read and learn on their own from mathematics texts and professional articles. The secret of the program's success is simply the department's commitment to providing a caring and nurturing environment.[8]

I offer this example both for its promise and as a caveat. While some might look to the case studies described herein as models or even blueprints for change, I would argue, paraphrasing Euclid, that there is no royal road to mounting a successful undergraduate program in science. Effective teaching can no more be independent of its environment than of its discipline. Take the laudable research experience offered students at many undergraduate institutions. While this works well in chemistry, physics does not lend itself as naturally to that kind of activity. As one physicist explained, not all physics is experimental, so teachers don't want to give their undergraduates the sense that it is. They also want to keep their majors from specializing too early. And, given the nature of research in the discipline, it is unlikely that undergraduate physics students can make much of a contribution before their final year. This does not mean one gives up on the idea of engaging students in some sort of quasi-professional activity. Rather that physics teachers need to invent an *equivalent experience* that will offer students the same thrill of discovery and sense of belonging that chemistry students at Fort Lewis, Trinity, University of Wisconsin-Eau Claire, and Cal State LA enjoy.

Similarly, the "less is more" approach of Ege and Laws may not suit every student or every faculty member or every undergraduate program, any more than all institutions can afford Dickinson's sophisticated computer-linked laboratory, or Case Western's fiber optics network for student-faculty communication. Resources have to be made available for projects that are suited to local conditions and local goals.

Where are these resources to come from? If money cannot "solve" the problem, surely resources–financial and other–can make some difference.

Resources for Cumulative Improvement—Four Pathways

The Howard Hughes Story

Beginning in 1988, the Howard Hughes Medical Institute suddenly became an important player in undergraduate science education reform. After completing negotiations with the IRS, the institute (not a founda-

---

[8] The same appears to be true for doctoral education in mathematics, according to an NRC report. See "Educating Mathematical Scientists: Doctoral Study and the Postdoctoral Experience in the United States," National Research Council, April 1992, as reviewed in *Nature 356*, 23 April 1992, p. 650.

tion, but rather a manager of medical research laboratories) agreed to grant $500 million over a ten-year period for any tax-exempt program consistent with its commitment to biomedical research and education. The officers and the trustees decided that the grants program would focus on science education, initially at the undergraduate and graduate levels. The goals of the undergraduate program were twofold: first, to increase the number and quality of biomedical programs at undergraduate institutions; second, to increase the number and proportion of undergraduates, including women and minorities underrepresented in the sciences, selecting biomedical research as a career. To begin, Joseph Perpich, vice president for grants and special programs, and Stephen Barkanic, program officer, analyzed data from the National Research Council and other sources on institutions graduating the highest proportion and number of future medical students and Ph.D.s in biology, chemistry, physics, and mathematics.

On the basis of this analysis, letters went out in 1987 to 100 private liberal arts, private comprehensive, and public and private historically minority institutions already doing a superb job of launching minority students into the biomedical sciences.[9] The targeted institutions (not individuals) were asked to design five-year plans in (1) undergraduate research; (2) curriculum, equipment, and laboratory facilities; (3) faculty development; and (4) outreach to elementary and secondary schools and community colleges. Forty-four awards ranging from $400,000 to $1.8 million were distributed the next year (for a total of $30.4 million). In 1989 and 1990 research and doctorate-granting institutions (public and private) were targeted and, by means of a similar procedure, $60 million was distributed to fifty-one. In 1991 the institute returned to small liberal arts, comprehensive, and minority institutions; in 1992 to the research universities. At Fort Lewis, a third-year recipient (because of Fort Lewis' American Indian population), Jim Mills recalls the department's delight both on winning an award and because of the manner in which the money was bestowed: the department was simply forwarded a check for $800,000 (which had been sent to Fort Lewis' president) to deposit against future needs as approved in the institute's grant.[10]

What is interesting about the Howard Hughes program is how very well it meshes with the lesson of the case studies presented here. The institute's purpose was institutional change and enlargement of oppor-

---

[9] Program announcements and annual reports from the Office of Grants and Special Programs, Howard Hughes Medical Institute, Bethesda, Md., 1988, 1989, 1990, 1991, 1992.

[10] Personal communication to the author. On a more modest level Research Corporation is employing the same strategy by selecting individual departments, one at a time, for overall institutional support against an invited five-year plan.

tunities. It targeted colleges and universities which had already demon-strated a capacity to produce minority graduates in the biomedical sciences, providing "post-performance rewards." *Its grants were not to individuals for experimentation, but to departments for improvement.* The specific line-items were general enough for each institution to tailor its spending to its own needs, and the time frame, in every instance, was five years–time enough to plan, implement, and assess.

The Pew Science Program in Undergraduate Education

Another model for cumulative improvement targets *clusters* of liberal arts colleges and research universities instead of individual programs, departments, or institutions of a single type. In 1988 the Pew Science Program in Undergraduate Education, funded by the Pew Charitable Trusts, began awarding three-year grants to such clusters of institutions, varying in size from six to sixteen schools over fairly large geographical areas, to undertake collaborative projects to improve undergraduate science education. The grants have ranged from $800,000 to $2.2 million, and have averaged about $50,000 per school per year. A cluster director (faculty member or academic administrator) and an executive council, composed of institutional representatives from the participating schools, do the planning for cluster activities and take primary responsibility for involving their individual science faculties in collaborative cluster projects.

The goal of the program is to revitalize undergraduate science educa-tion at the 72 participating colleges and universities. "The insistence on collaboration among schools," says Joan Girgus, executive director, is to guarantee that "for every problem tackled, there will be a critical mass of interested faculty to encourage one another and to engage in joint problem solving;" also to leverage resources so that "while each science department will have to be fully engaged for maximum benefit to occur, no one department will have to find all the necessary resources for reform within itself;" and, finally, to allow faculty to choose that aspect of the program they find most appealing. The hope, says Girgus, quoting a member of her National Advisory Committee, is not modest. Pew wants to "change the culture of science" in participating schools.[11]

Much of the work of the clusters has so far centered on curriculum projects involving faculty (and students) from as few as two and as many as ten schools. Clusters sponsor workshops and conferences on research as well as curricular and pedagogical topics. The grants also provide summer support enabling students to work as members of faculty

---

[11] Joan Girgus, executive director of the Pew Science Program in Undergraduate Educa-tion, in a personal communication to the author.

research teams at any of the cluster institutions. These culminate in cluster-wide end-of-summer conferences at which students present their work. Mindful that some undergraduates headed for science are not yet able to contribute to faculty research, some clusters have devised special summer programs for first-year students and for students in mathematics and computer science.

The funding provided by Pew is not intended to create new dependencies—this time at the cluster level; rather, says the director, to help reformers locate like-minded colleagues on a regional level and get the local reforms they want under way. To this end, Pew now requires clusters to contribute 10 percent of the direct costs in the second year of funding and 20 percent in the third year. The intent is to make clear that institutions are going to have to pick up the continuing costs of cluster activities and the ongoing costs of whatever reforms may evolve. Only time will tell whether Pew's leverage model produces lasting change where other less imaginative funding has failed.

Designating Indirect Costs for Undergraduate Science

Where else might institutional development monies come from? During the past forty years the government agencies which support science research have allowed host institutions to claim indirect costs and overhead to support their research infrastructure. Sometimes they are returned by the college or university administration to the department which initiated the funded project. More often than not, however, the monies are applied to general institutional expenses. Iowa State University at Ames is trying to change the way these funds are allocated. The university already returns 15 percent of indirect costs to the principal investigator. A proposal to return an additional 25 percent to the department is currently before the vice president for finance.

While there is no legal prohibition against designating such funds for undergraduate instruction, pressure from research scientists makes this unlikely unless there is counter pressure. Federal research dollars could directly support undergraduate science, says Bernard White, chair of biochemistry at Iowa State, if it were mandated that a certain share of indirect costs be applied to improving instruction, much in the way the Howard Hughes money was allocated to be used as each department sees fit. At the very least, the funding agency could require that principal investigators be involved in undergraduate teaching.

Wrenching Resources from Quasi-Instructional Services

In a period of downsizing, and with government and foundation funding primarily dedicated to innovation and the search for and testing of universal solutions, it may be necessary to look closer to home for ways of transferring existing resources into funds for improvement. A first step might be for instructional units (departments, divisions, colleges) to *reclaim* some of the many quasi-instructional budget lines that, over the past several decades, have been arrogated by institutional administrations. Today such resources are consumed by student affairs, academic affairs, career placement, and institutional research (even the registrar), offices that assist with advising, course and program registration, room assignment, instructional improvement, instructional assessment, academic support activities, financial aid, and career placement, to note but a few.

One small example of this kind of change indicates how potent such a strategy might be. Recently the Department of Biology at the University of Illinois-Chicago created a full-time position out of half a faculty line and some Howard Hughes money to work exclusively on undergraduate affairs. The new staff member, who holds an undergraduate minor in biology and has six years counseling experience at the college level, occupies an office in biology, open from nine to five, and sees majors, prospective majors, even students outside of biology who, for one reason or another, are enrolled in biology courses at this large, urban institution. The staff member signs program cards, controls drop and add petitions, sets up appointments with faculty for students who might not do this on their own, and conducts surveys and investigations of issues that individual instructors or the department itself want researched. From such conversations and investigations, this staff member is able to provide ongoing feedback and advice to faculty about particular courses, and to the department chair about the biology program as a whole. The adviser is more than an adviser; she has become a valued participant in meetings on the department's undergraduate instructional functions. The position is valuable precisely because the department defines the job and it is to the department that the staff member reports.

While the biology chairman has been unable (as this was written) to wrench the position away from university-wide student services, he firmly believes that it should be rooted in the department and that funding should come from existing resources. He intends to lobby for funding to maintain the post in biology when the Hughes grant expires.

Imagine every college or university science department with its own office of undergraduate affairs. Imagine a staff of academic professionals–its numbers depending on the size of the institution, the number of students served in lower division courses, and the number of majors– who keep abreast of institutional reform in other institutions and assist locally with program assessment and improvement. Imagine useful and usable feedback mechanisms linking students with faculty, faculty with one another and with the department chair, all under department aegis and control (in policy language, "site-managed").

So long as quasi-instructional services continue to be centralized the special needs of science students and departments will be shortchanged. Student services are rarely science-oriented, if for no other reason than few of those who provide them are science graduates. The special requirements of laboratory courses may not be understood by people who have not taken or taught laboratory courses. The costs of educating students in science, both financial and in terms of faculty load and student course credit, may not be properly assessed. When these decisions are returned to the departments of science, it will be possible for those who wish to do a better job of teaching to do so.

Wrenching resources is an exercise in power, and it's likely that some scientists will have neither the skills nor the stomach for it. As others have noted before me, college faculty in all fields, not just in the sciences, tend to confuse autonomy with power. They are grateful that, once they shut their classroom door, they can do more or less what they want. But in fact many of the constraints on instructional improvement–not to mention instruction itself–are not within their control: the kind and number of students who enroll; the course credit allocated for the work they require; room size; the quality of their TAs; and grading assistance and support. If instruction is to again become the responsibility of the science department, then the means to do the job must be taken, not just from add-on resources, but from the very heart of the college or university budget.

If federal stipends were available for students willing to complete a major in science, engineering, or mathematics; if indirect costs were returned to departments for instructional improvement; and if some resources and personnel lines were taken from quasi-instructional student services, I believe many more students would be attracted to science and would be better served by the major whatever their ultimate career. Then faculty members with worthy reforms–faculty like David Layzer, Dudley Herschbach, and Eric Mazur at Harvard, like Barbara Sawrey and Paul Saltman at UCSD, like Tony Andreoli and Carlos Gutierrez at Cal State LA, and like all the other change agents we have encountered– could make cumulative improvement the rule and not the exception.

One can only applaud Congress' willingness to increase funding for science education reform, and the growing commitment of a number of federal agencies–NSF, and the Departments of Education and Energy–to that same goal.[12] But unless and until means are found to *mainstream* and *manage* change, the nation is at risk (to borrow Gerald Holton's phrase) of having to launch still another campaign a decade from now.

---

[12] *Nature*, (1991) "U.S. Budget: NSF Wins, Space Science Loses," Vol. 353, 3 October, p. 372.

Measuring Change

In selecting a set of programs to describe in this volume, I imposed my own intuitive list of "desirable outcomes"–recruitment, retention, and high morale–and my own judgment as to how well certain programs and/or courses were meeting those outcomes. In so doing, I borrowed heavily from department and course designers' own local goals and measures. But my outcomes were no more systematically arrived at than theirs. Hence "success" remains a matter of judgment and interpretation–theirs and mine, and now the readers'. Is that good enough? I think not. Researching and writing this book have led me to believe that those who would reform science teaching at college need to engage in a process of *planning and evaluation*, however unfamiliar (and unpalatable) that process may be.

How else will faculty members, department chairs, deans, and the public at large know whether change in undergraduate science teaching is in "the direction of the good," as the Japanese put it; that is, how well (or poorly) any program is meeting some set of goals?

It is wrong to assume that "evaluation" is nothing more than testing, followed by statistically simple comparisons between institutions and/ or cohorts. There was a time when some target population would be identified, measured at two points in time (before and after intervention), and objectively compared to a similar population that did not have the benefits of the program. Though superficially "scientific," such findings did not provide useful feedback (called "formative evaluation" as against "summative evaluation"–the finding of cause and effect). As the late Marcia Guttentag argued in her critique of classical evaluation techniques, "Program administrators have goals not hypotheses, and programs are the inverse of the carefully designed single variables of the experimental paradigm."[13]

In recent years, professional evaluators have moved away from the quasi-experimental approach.[14] If the appropriate model of science education reform is a process model, the model for evaluation must also emphasize process. Working scientists have every right to demand that any system of program planning and evaluation meet their own standards of validity and reliability; provide useful and usable feedback; and offer specific guidance for future action. Evaluation need not be done by experts. A more appropriate approach, as the case studies suggest, can

---

[13] Marcia Guttentag, "Subjectivity and its Use in Evaluation Research," *Evaluation*, 1:2, 1973, p. 60.

[14] See, for example, the writings of Michael Quinn Patton, *Practical Evaluation* and *Creative Evaluation* both published by Sage Publications in 1982 and 1987 respectively.

be initiated by insiders who try to find some agreement among themselves as to what they would like to achieve, given certain extra efforts. Achievement, in this model, is measured not against raw outcomes, but in terms of departmental expectations and goals. Such an approach involves the faculty at every stage of goal-setting, assessment is essentially self-evaluation, and the purpose of the exercise is to give the faculty feedback as to what works and what doesn't.

Scientists are in an enviable position to invent and apply their own planning and evaluation techniques. For one, they will be very canny in employing statistical inference. For another, their own research orientation makes them doggedly empirical. All that's lacking is to decide *what constitutes achievement and when is the appropriate time to measure it.*

The faculty responsible for the courses and programs described in this volume seem to have intuitively subscribed to this philosophy in setting goals and measuring outcomes. When, for example, the chemistry faculty at UW-Eau Claire decided to revive their curriculum committee in the face of general satisfaction with their program, they were asking for an opportunity to assess what they were doing and to develop guidelines for future action. The success of the first cohort of structure and reactivity students at Michigan, who have just completed their third year, will be measured not by artificial means, but by the most obvious: success in upper-level courses, graduation rates, and career choices upon graduation. These may be the only meaningful evaluations that can be made of Ege's program.

Summing Up

There are many other exemplary courses and programs in physical science at the nation's colleges and universities that could have been included here. The intent was not to provide a comprehensive survey, but rather to look for common features in the way science faculty in certain institutions are struggling to revitalize instruction. That process, as the narratives surely demonstrate, is *sui generis*, each locale having its own definition of success, its own means of moving toward its goals. Still, while local initiatives and local control are to be cherished, there is no point in every science department having to start from scratch. Some degree of coordination, certainly communication, is desirable. Travel, teaching postdoctoral fellowships, visiting faculty, and faculty exchanges need to be supported.[15] But nothing can replace the vision, the leadership,

---

[15] Pew's consortium model (see p. 164) is intended to encourage faculty exchange and communication.

and the hard work that characterize programs that succeed.

Harvard and Cal State LA are separated by more than a continent. Michigan has nearly as many students in introductory chemistry as Fort Lewis will see in six years. Trinity University is sending more and more chemistry majors on to Ph.D. programs. Paul Saltman wants to eliminate elementary teachers' dread of science. Yet, reformers in all the places described in this volume subscribe to a single working premise (in the terms of Daniel Sullivan of Project Kaleidoscope, a "compelling vision"), namely, that every institution is responsible for advancing the scientific power of all students who enroll, no matter how well or poorly prepared they may be, how well or poorly motivated. Since different institutions enroll very different kinds of students, it is not very likely that any single national model will be as effective as local strategies for accomplishing local aims. But what must become universal is, to quote Sullivan again, the *will* to make things better.

Appendices

The University of Michigan
Undergraduate Chemistry Curriculum

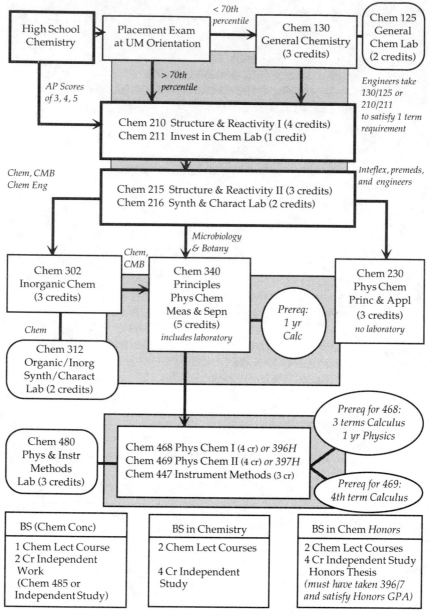

CMB=Cellular and Molecular Biology
A combined Chem/Chem Eng Degree option and a Chem Educ option are also available

The University of Michigan
Sample Examinations, Structure and Reactivity

Rather than asking them for the recapitulation of some particular set of facts, students are provided with primary data (such as one would obtain in the laboratory). An appropriate concept must be identified as well as applied in order to *solve* the problem at hand. The particular examples represented in this problem were *necessarily* **not** among the examples used to illustrate the concept in the lecture.

Note that students are required to provide both textual and pictorial representations for phenomena. Multiple representations allow for a cross-check on student understanding that is not possible when only a recollection and identification are called for.

SECOND EXAMINATION, *CHEMISTRY 210*, OCTOBER 31, 1989

v. (22 points)

The potency of an anesthetic has been found to be related to the extent to which it disrupts hydrogen bonding in nerve cell membranes. This capacity to disrupt hydrogen bonding is related to the *acidity* of *carbon-hydrogen bonds* and to the *basicity* of *oxygen atoms* in the compounds used as anesthetics. Three widely used anesthetics were examined. They are shown below.

CF_3CHClB_r	$CH_3OCF_2CHCl_2$	CHF_2OCF_2CHFCl
halothane	methoxyflurane	enflurane

1. Halothane has pK_a 23.8. What is the approximate pK_a that you would expect for ethane?

Explain in a few words and with structural representations why the acidity of halothane differs from that of ethane.

2. Methoxyflurane has two possible sites of deprotonation. The researchers found that only one site was deprotonated under the conditions of their reaction. Write a structural formula for the more stable of the two possible conjugate bases of methoxyflurane.

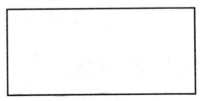

3. Methoxyflurane is 10 times more potent than enflurane as an anesthetic even though both compounds have approximately the same pK_a, ~26. According to the criteria listed at the beginning of this question, why should methoxyflurane be more potent than enflurane? Explain in a few words and with structural representations.

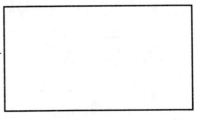

Contemporary applications that illustrate fundamental chemistry phenomena are not hard to find. Instructors can avail themselves of the wide variety of examples found in recent journals. Formulating questions from new observations helps the instructor to avoid the traps of recycling the same old examples in a different form, and perhaps of inventing chemistry that might not actually be true! Quite to the contrary, this technique allows us to include all the novel ways that scientists other than ourselves look at chemistry. After all, this is the real skill that we have developed as professionals: the ability to look at new and unfamiliar science and make sense of it in the context of our broader conceptual understanding.

THIRD EXAMINATION, *CHEMISTRY 210*, JUNE 18, 1991
I. (17 points)

Generally, the two different enantiomeric forms of a substance show different biological activity. Recently, a group of chemists from Copenhagen prepared the enantiomer of the molecule called AZT, which is used in the treatment of AIDS, in order to see whether or not it might be an even better drug for treatment of the disease *(J. Org. Chem. 1991, 56, 3591- 3594).*

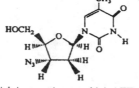

(+)-AZT used in treatment

$[\alpha]^{20}_D = +56°(1.0g/100mL\ CH_3OH)$

a) Draw (-)-AZT, which is enantiomer of (+)-AZT:

b) Use an arrow to clearly point to all stereocenters in your (-)-AZT structure and provide configurational assignments.

9

c) What is the specific rotation of (-)-AZT expected to be?

2

d) What total number of stereoisomers are possible for the AZT connectivity?

2

e) The following reaction is used to join the two rings together in preparing AZT.

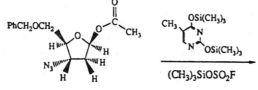

$(CH_3)_3SiOSO_2F$

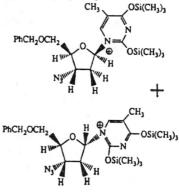

+

What sort of reaction mechanism is implied by this experimental result? Give a specific mechanism classification and a reason for your selection.

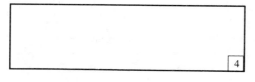

4

Students are consistently exposed to the rich variety of contexts associated with structural chemistry. In this example from the second term of the course, some important ideas from biomedical research form the basis of a synthetic chemistry problem. The message is clear: advancements in this area of science are integrated with an ability to prepare and design new molecules.

By always seeking out examples from the scientific literature, it is possible to illustrate the exciting multiculture of modern chemistry. For example, on the page following this question on biomedical chemistry there was a problem dealing with transition metal coordination chemistry.

THIRD EXAMINATION, *CHEMISTRY 215,* APRIL 3, 1990

v. (22 points)

One potential method for tumor treatment being proposed is to covalently attach clusters of boron atoms (as $B_{10}H_{10}$) to antibodies that target the cancer cells. Neutron activation of the boron atoms would cause α-particle emission that would be lethal to the neighboring cancer cells *(F. Hawthorne, J. Org.Chem. 1990, 55, 838-843).*

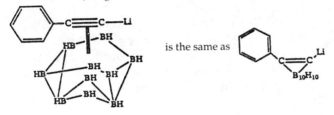

Complete the following sequence.

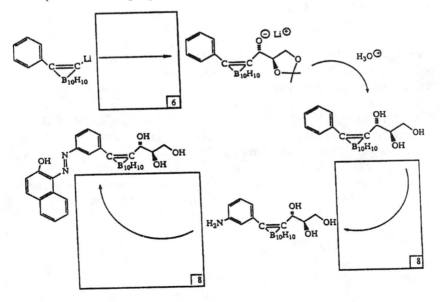

University of Utah
Syllabus for the First Two Years of Chemistry

First Quarter: *Chem. 161 E (5 hr) Introduction to Chemistry* –Topics: matter and its properties, atomic theory, molecules and ions, the mole concept, chemical formulas, chemical equations, electronic structure including quantum background, periodic table development, enthalpy and the First Law of Thermodynamics, gases, liquids and solids, solutions.

Second Quarter: *Chem. 162 E (5 hr) Structure and Bonding of Molecules I (Organic)* –Topics: Bonding–ionic and covalent, shapes and polarity, orbitals including bond strengths, acids and bases including pKa and equilibrium, reaction pathways including kinetics, transition state, activation energy concepts, alkanes, stereochemistry, nucleophilic and elimination reactions, alkenes, electrophilic addition, carbocation concept, alkynes.

Third Quarter: *Chem. 163 E (5 hr) Properties and Reaction Mechanisms of Molecules (Organic)* –Topics: infrared and nuclear magnetic resonance, spectroscopy, alcohols and ethers, oxidation and reduction, aldehydes and ketones, carboxylic acids, nucleophilic reactions of the carbonyl group, synthetic transformations, enolate ions and their reactions.

Fourth Quarter: *Chem. 261 E (5 hr) Reactions and Synthesis of Molecules (Organic)* –Topics: aromatic chemistry, electrophilic substitution, free radicals, amines, heterocyclic compounds, carbohydrates, amino acids and proteins.

Fifth Quarter: *Chem. 262 E (4 hr) Chemical Equilibria* –Topics: introduction to quantitative equilibrium concepts, acids, bases, buffers, oxidation, reduction, entropy and free energy, electrochemistry.

Sixth Quarter: *Chem. 263 E (5 hr) Structure and Bonding of Molecules II (Inorganic)* –Topics: chemistry of the periodic table, non-metals, metals, coordination chemistry, inorganic stereochemistry, introduction to crystal field theory, inorganic spectroscopy, some special topics such as organometallic compounds, catalysis, boron chemistry, atmospheric chemistry, nuclear chemistry.

Harvard University
Courses of Instruction (1992-1993)
Draft Catalog Entries for Chem 8/9 and Math 28/29

Chemistry 8. Matter, Energy, and Equilibrium. The atomic hypothesis. Energy and its transformations. Entropy and free energy. Dissociative, phase, and chemical equilibria. Statistical theory of thermodynamic equilibrium.

Chemistry 8, Chemistry 9, Mathematics 28, and Mathematics 29 offer a unified introduction to basic principles in classical mechanics, quantum physics and chemistry, and statistical physics and chemistry, and to the mathematical language needed to express and apply these principles. The courses are intended for both concentrators and nonconcentrators in the physical and biological sciences.

Taken together, Chemistry 8 and Chemistry 9 satisfy the same requirements as, and cannot be counted for credit in addition to, Physics 15a and Chemistry 10. Mathematics 28 and 29 satisfy the same requirements as, and cannot be counted for credit in addition to, Mathematics 21ab.

Format. Emphasizes active learning in a cooperative, noncompetitive, and interactive environment. Meets in discussion sections with 15 or fewer students. The sections have common reading and writing assignments. Students are encouraged to work together in smaller study groups. Grading is based on an assessment of the quality of the student's written work and of his or her contributions to the classroom discussions, considered in the light of his or her mathematical and scientific background.

Laboratories. Five two-hour laboratories, intended to help students anchor theoretical concepts in experience and to recreate crucial experiments.

Prerequisites. An understanding of basic concepts of the calculus and a strong background in physics and chemistry at the high-school level. Simultaneous enrollment in Mathematics 28 is required except for students who can demonstrate a mastery of the subject matter of that course.

Enrollment. Limited to 30. M, W, F 9; lab meetings to be arranged.

Chemistry 9. Atomic and Molecular Structure and Processes. A continuation of Chemistry 8. Rate processes (chemical kinetics, masers and lasers, approach to equilibrium). Classical underpinnings of quantum physics. Schroedinger's equation. Electron spin and the Pauli principle. The minimum energy principle. Applications to atomic and molecular structure.

Laboratories. Five two-hour laboratories, intended to help students anchor theoretical concepts in experience and to recreate crucial experiments.

Prerequisites. Chemistry 8. Simultaneous enrollment in Mathematics 29 is required except for students who can demonstrate a mastery of the subject matter of that course.

M, W, F 9; lab meetings to be arranged.

Mathematics 28. Practicum in Advanced Calculus. Mathematical foundations of classical particle physics and thermodynamics: Taylor series, vectors and their rates of change, scalar and vector fields, line integrals, partial derivatives, probability theory, Lagrange multipliers.

Explores in depth the mathematical concepts and theories that figure most prominently in Chemistry 8. Open to students not enrolled in Chemistry 8 as space permits.

Format. The courses emphasize active learning in a cooperative, noncompetitive, and interactive environment. Each of the courses is given entirely in discussion sections with 15 or fewer students. The sections have common reading and writing assignments. Students are encouraged to work together in smaller study groups. Grading is based on an assessment of the quality of the student's written work and of his or her contributions to the classroom discussions, considered in the light of his or her mathematical and scientific background.

Prerequisites. An understanding of basic concepts of the calculus and a strong background in physics and chemistry at the high school level.

Enrollment. Limited to 30. Tu, Th 9-10:30

Mathematics 29. Practicum in Advanced Calculus. Mathematical aspects of rate processes, classical dynamics, waves, and quantum mechanics: Ordinary differential equations (dynamical systems) and their integrals; eigenvalue problems in one, two, and three dimensions; Fourier series and integrals; introduction to Hilbert spaces.

Explores in depth the mathematical concepts and theories that figure most prominently in Chemistry 9. Open to students not enrolled in Chemistry 9 as space permits.

Format. The courses emphasize active learning in a cooperative, noncompetitive, and interactive environment. Each of the courses is given entirely in discussion sections with 15 or fewer students. The sections have common reading and writing assignments. Students are encouraged to work together in smaller study groups. Grading is based on an assessment of the quality of the student's written work and of his or her contributions to the classroom discussions, considered in the light of his or her mathematical and scientific background.

Prerequisites. Mathematics 28 or equivalent.

Enrollment. Limited to 30.

Tu, Th 9-10:30

About the Author

Sheila Tobias has made a science and an art of being a curriculum outsider. Neither a mathematician nor a scientist, she has tackled the question of why intelligent and motivated college students have task-specific disabilities in certain disciplines, particularly mathematics and science. From her work have come four books prior to this one on science and mathematics: *Overcoming Math Anxiety* (1978), *Succeed with Math* (1987), *They're Not Dumb, They're Different: Stalking the Second Tier* (1990), and (with physicist Carl T. Tomizuka) *Breaking the Science Barrier* (1992). She is the creator of the technique, "Peer Perspectives on Teaching," in which faculty from fields other than science and mathematics "stand in" for students in artificially constructed science and mathematics lessons at the college level. From their responses to the instruction have come important insights into what makes science and mathematics "hard" and even "distasteful" for outsiders.

Educated in history and literature at Harvard-Radcliffe and Columbia Universities, Ms. Tobias has been a lecturer in history and political science at the Universities of Arizona and of California, San Diego, a college administrator at Cornell and Wesleyan Universities, and a trustee of Stephens College, a woman's college in Columbia, Mo. Her work in science and mathematics avoidance and anxiety has been funded by the Lilly Endowment, the Rockefeller and Ford Foundations, and the Fund for the Improvement of Postsecondary Education in the Department of Education, as well as by Research Corporation.

Selected Bibliography

Overcoming Math Anxiety (W.W. Norton, 1978, Houghton Mifflin paperback, 1980; new edition in press). *Succeed with Math: Every Student's Guide to Conquering Math Anxiety* (The College Board, 1987). *They're Not Dumb, They're Different: Stalking the Second Tier* (Research Corporation, 1990). *Breaking the Science Barrier*, with Carl T. Tomizuka (The College Board, 1992).

Articles on math anxiety: *MS* magazine, September, 1976; *The Atlantic*, September 1978; *Harvard Educational Review*, Vol. 50, No. 1, Spring 1980; *Psychology Today*, January 1982; *Physics Today*, Vol. 38, No. 6, June 1985. Articles on teaching science: *Change* magazine, Spring 1986; *The Physics Teacher*, Vol. 26, No. 2, February 1988; *American Journal of Physics*, 56 (9), September 1988; *American Journal of Physics*, September 1990; *Physics Today*, November 1990. On educational reform: Distinguished Lecture in the Social Sciences, Northern Illinois University, November 15, 1990; *The American Journal of Pharmaceutical Education*, 55, Winter 1991; *The Sciences*, January/February 1991; *The Chronicle of Higher Education*, January 1991; *The Scientist*, February 1991. Also articles on the same subject in *Change* magazine, May/June 1992; *Journal of Science Education and Technology*, June 1992.

The Rapporteurs for This Study

Sylvia Teich Horowitz, California State University, Los Angeles

Sylvia Teich Horowitz is a graduate of Brooklyn College and received her Ph.D. in chemistry from Columbia University. She has taught organic and biological chemistry at California State University, Los Angeles for more than twenty years. Her research interests include steroid biochemistry, the metabolism of glucosamine and its polymers and, more recently, nutritional aspects of biochemistry. With coauthors Robert M. McAllister, M.D. and Raymond V. Bilden, Ph.D., she is working on a book dealing with the molecular biology of cancer. She has long been interested in the history of women in science and in ways of recruiting more women and other underrepresented groups into the field.

Abigail Lipson, Harvard University

Abigail Lipson, Ph.D. is a clinical psychologist and senior member of Harvard University's Bureau of Study Counsel. She is the author, with Harvard colleague David N. Perkins, of *Block: The Psychology of Counterintentional Behavior in Everyday Life* (Lyle Stuart, 1990), contributed a chapter to *They're Not Dumb, They're Different: Stalking the Second Tier*, and writes widely on motivation, achievement, cognitive development, and education. She also maintains a private practice in Cambridge, Massachusetts.

Patricia A. Moore, University of California, San Diego

Patricia A. Moore holds a doctorate in education administration and for ten years has been working in education at the University of California, San Diego, where she now directs grant-funded teacher enhancement programs. In addition, she is adjunct faculty at the University of Redlands and the University of LaVerne, a grant writer for nonprofit organizations, and a career consultant. She spent ten years teaching overseas in a variety of countries to diverse cultural groups.

Stella Pagonis, University of Wisconsin-Eau Claire

Stella Pagonis holds bachelor's and master's degrees in Information Science from the University of Pittsburgh. For eighteen years she worked in strategic planning, corporate development, and marketing management in large corporate environments including Gulf Oil, Control Data, and Northern Telecom. She currently consults in marketing, market planning, and marketing research for small and medium-sized companies in Wisconsin, specializing in strategic planning, corporate development, marketing research, product management, marketing management, and sales. She is married to Warren Gallagher, and a member of the chemistry department at University of Wisconsin-Eau Claire.

Suzan Potuznik, University of California, San Diego

Suzan Potuznik began her science training with the aim of becoming an oceanographer. After studying geology, physics, and chemistry, she completed her Ph.D. in organometallic chemistry at the University of California, San Diego, abandoning oceanography for chemistry. She is currently a visiting assistant professor in chemistry at the University of San Diego.

Brian P. Coppola, University of Michigan

Brian P. Coppola is lecturer in chemistry at the University of Michigan and the coordinator for the undergraduate organic curriculum. He received his B.S. in chemistry from the University of New Hampshire, and his Ph.D. in organic chemistry from the University of Wisconsin-Madison. From 1982-1986, he was an assistant professor of chemistry at the University of Wisconsin-Whitewater, and in 1986 joined the faculty at Michigan where he has worked with Seyhan Ege on the design and implementation of the new undergraduate chemistry curriculum. Dr. Coppola also collaborates with the Center for Research on Learning and Teaching and the Center for the Education of Women at Michigan, where he is designing the evaluation component of the new program. In addition, he is involved in preservice teacher training and precollege curriculum development–all in science.

Margaret Bartlett, Fort Lewis College

Margaret Bartlett has been working and associating with scientists for some twenty-seven years. Her BA in sociology from Luther College prepared her for a career in social work and preschool teaching. She has more than a decade of activism in measuring and promoting the effectiveness of public K-12 education. Some of her knowledge of the chemistry program at Fort Lewis comes through her student and alumni friends and through her spouse, Ted Bartlett.

Katya Fels, Harvard University

Katya Fels, now a senior biochemistry major at Harvard, was a freshman when she took chem-phys and a sophomore when she served as undergraduate discussion leader for the course. With physicists for parents, Katya already knew science could be an exciting and creative pursuit when she came to college. She claims this knowledge helped her maintain her commitment to science during some dry, extremely difficult introductory science courses.

Steve Brenner, Harvard University

Steve Brenner, a senior biochemistry major at Harvard, took chem-phys as a freshman, and served as participant-observer in the course the following year. Before college it was his father, a physicist, and a few inspiring grade school science teachers who encouraged his early, wide-ranging interest in science.

David Hall, Harvard University

David Hall is a graduate student in physics at Harvard, where he teaches physics 11 and works in a laboratory in addition to taking classes. He began his education at Amherst College thinking he would study a humanities discipline, but an introductory physics class his freshman year was so good he changed his mind. He received a B.S. in physics from Amherst in 1991. He hopes to combine teaching, equipment work, and physical research as a professor of physics at a small undergraduate institution.

K. Wayne Yang , Harvard University

K. Wayne Yang is a graduating senior in physics at Harvard and one of Harvard's few undergraduate teaching assistants. He plans to teach physics in an inner-city high school in either Los Angeles or Oakland, California after graduation.

About Research Corporation
A Foundation for the Advancement of Science

One of the first U.S. foundations and the only one wholly devoted to the advancement of science, Research Corporation was established in 1912 by scientist, inventor and philanthropist Frederick Gardner Cottrell with the assistance of Charles Doolittle Walcott, secretary of the Smithsonian Institution. Its objectives: to make inventions "more available and effective in the useful arts and manufactures," and "to provide means for the advancement and extension of technical and scientific investigation, research and experimentation. . . ."

Cottrell's inspiration–he was a physical chemist at the University of California–was to create Research Corporation to develop his invention, the electrostatic precipitator for controlling air pollution, and other discoveries from universities, and devote any monies realized to awards for scholarly research.

Research Corporation awards support scientific inquiry in physics, chemistry and astronomy at public and private undergraduate institutions (Cottrell College Science Awards); assist midcareer chemists, astronomers and physicists in Ph.D.-granting university science departments (Research Opportunity Awards); and support promising research, programs and prizes not falling under other programs (General Foundation Awards). A fourth program, Partners In Science, aims to improve high school science education by giving secondary teachers opportunities to do summer research at local colleges and universities.

Grants applications from college and university scientists are reviewed by referees suggested by applicants and supplemented, as appropriate, by the foundation. A final reading of applications and recommendations for approval or denial is given by an advisory committee of academic scientists. Research Corporation awards are supported by an endowment created by the sale of the electrostatic precipitation business, and by donations from other foundations, industrial companies and individuals wishing to advance academic science.

The research which led to *Revitalizing Undergraduate Science: Why Some Things Work and Most Don't*, is responsive to a Research Corporation goal, formulated in 1987, "to increase the flow of young people into the sciences with programs appropriate to the foundation's interest and expertise." A previous study, *They're Not Dumb, They're Different: Stalking the Second Tier*, was published in 1990. Research Corporation will consider for publication other papers that are especially relevant to the advancement of science and science education.

Research Corporation's office is located at 6840 East Broadway Boulevard, Tucson, Arizona 85710-2815.

Index